This guidebook will teach you the vocabulary and grammar of the language of success. You will learn . . .

- how to create a *positive* climate in your interactions with others—with magical results!

- why giving others what they most want (your support) is the surest way of getting whatever you want!

- why *listening* is your most important communication tool, and how you can become that rare person—the good listener.

- the dangers of saying too much.

- the importance of knowing how to handle *silence* in a conversation—and how you can benefit from it.

- how to read the other person's mood.

- how to recognize hidden messages.

- why you must learn to recognize "hotbuttons" —what they are and why you should always look for them . . .

Speak the Language of Success

GLORIA HOFFMAN and
PAULINE GRAIVIER
As told to Jane Phillips

B
BERKLEY BOOKS, NEW YORK

This Berkley book contains the complete
text of the original hardcover edition.
It has been completely reset in a typeface
designed for easy reading and was printed
from new film.

SPEAK THE LANGUAGE OF SUCCESS

A Berkley Book / published by arrangement with
G. P. Putnam's Sons

PRINTING HISTORY
G. P. Putnam's Sons edition 1983
Jove edition / January 1985
Berkley edition / October 1986
Special Sales Edition / March 1992

A BERKLEY BOOK ® TM 757,375
Berkley Books are published by The Berkley Publishing Group,
200 Madison Avenue, New York, NY 10016.
The name "BERKLEY" and the stylized "B" with design
are trademarks belonging to Berkley Publishing Corporation.

PRINTED IN THE UNITED STATES OF AMERICA

To our husbands and children
    Harold & Len
    Richard
    Robert
    Lisa
    Shelley
    Miles
    Tracy
    Roma
    Jeremy
You're the proof that it works.

Contents

Introduction

There are certain secrets of success to everything in life—tricks of the trade we all pick up as we go along, no matter what our occupation or profession, our routine or personal pursuits. Somewhere along the way we discover there's a faster way to change a tire, a better way to build a mousetrap, a more efficient way to distribute the sales force and so on.

You can sum up all these successful secrets, these tricks of the trade (whatever the trade may be), in one word: *experience*. If you do anything often enough or long enough, sooner or later you'll learn how to do it faster or better. We all learn by doing. With one exception. Surprisingly, that exception is the one "trade" we all have in common, the one daily pursuit in which we all have more accumulated experience than we'll ever gain in any other area of our lives: *communication*.

We communicate all day, every day. From the moment we open our eyes in the morning, the day's talk show is under way. But from the sound of things, even all that experience has left some of the secrets of success

1

in this particular field safely tucked away in *someone else's* vocabulary.

What is it about communicating that seems to come so easily for some and remain such a mystery for the rest of us? What fine tuning have they discovered that we don't hear? Why do some people's words seem to get them whatever they want, while we're still trying to describe to the plumber that the thingamabob that fits on the what'sit doesn't seem to be working, and even though we know he closed seven minutes ago, would he consider letting us pay him overtime to come out anyway?

Why is it that all those television anchorpersons and talk-show hosts (and even their guests) never seem to lose the thread of what they're saying; never drop the conversational ball with a thud; never have to say they're sorry; and *always* have a witty comeback for even the most inane remark? Why are we always left with a mouthful of verbal cartoons?

Communicating *is* like any other trade; it *does* have trade secrets. But unlike most of life's other occupations, we usually find ourselves too occupied with just talking our way through the day to consider the value of our verbal investments until we hear that our stock just dropped. The windfall profits of being able to communicate effectively—in any walk and talk of life—are available to everyone. *You* can win with your words. *You* can hold your own with the best. *You* can speak the language of success and talk your way right to the top. Others have done it; why not *you?*

Winning with words is the most valuable and marketable skill of the world you live in. Skillful communication is *the* secret of succeeding in the eighties.

The world is waiting for people who speak the language of success; people who are confident of what they have to offer, know their assets and can communicate those assets with confidence.

Pick up any newspaper and look at the ads: opportunity is everywhere. The world you live in takes its talkmasters seriously and seeks them out for every opportunity it offers.

If you can win with words—communicate confidently with people at every level, motivate and lead with your words—you can write your own ticket in the eighties.

You're holding the book that will tell you how to speak the language of success. Not a lecture, not a textbook, this is an actual, practical guide, the word-for-word way to do it. We don't deal in theories or mythful thinking. We present a full-length conversation about what will work and what won't, and why. We give you the method, the real how-to that you want to hear.

Realistically, if you're anything like the rest of us, you're thinking, Okay, fine. Maybe I will get good at this, but if I don't get an opportunity to use it, how can I succeed? I mean, I've been waiting all my life to be in the right place at the right time . . . and I'm still here. You have to get the breaks. I never even won a football pool at the office!

Fair enough. That's why we introduce you to the language of success by its first name, so to speak, in the first chapter. The first three "winning words" in its vocabulary are: *opportunity, confidence* and *assets*. That's where this conversation begins.

To make your verbal investments pay off in the business world, you'll need to meet opportunity face to face. And meeting it is a surprising introduction indeed.

· 1 ·

The Business of
Opportunity (Be at Home
When It Knocks)

"Been waiting long?" he asked casually, joining the cluster of people on the corner.

"For a while, I guess," said the fellow next to him.

"When is it due?" the newcomer continued.

"Don't know."

Raising his voice a bit and leaning forward to take in the entire group with his next question, the now slightly irritated latecomer inquired plaintively, "Doesn't *anybody* know when the bus is due?"

A woman who had been listening to the increasingly frustrating exchange commented stoically, "Nobody knows when it's due. Nobody has a schedule. We're all just waiting till it shows up."

Standing on the corner waiting for the bus, hoping it's the right time for it to come by, is like waiting for the right time to go on a diet—it never seems to come. It's like waiting for opportunity to knock. It never seems to.

Figuratively speaking, many of us have spent more time than we'd like to admit getting all dressed up and sitting on the proverbial parlor sofa, waiting for op-

4

portunity to come courting, to seek us out, to knock the door down.

Don't expect opportunity to come looking for you. As one man laughingly summed it up, "Opportunity's like Lady Luck—flirtatious, and often fickle. She's broken more than one appointment with me."

Like luck, opportunity seems to take pride in a dual strategy of subtlety and coquettish appeal. But opportunity doesn't always play fair.

Success is a pretty straight shooter, a good sport. You learn your game well enough and success will say "Okay, come on over. Let's play doubles." Success is a realist.

But opportunity is the perennial flirt, never being where you expect, playing the romantic.

We're here to tell you there's about as much romance in waiting for opportunity to knock as there is in waiting for a bus. The romance of opportunity is only in romantic fiction. You may find opportunity knocking at castle doors, but don't expect to find it at the office. That's not to say, however, that there *isn't* any opportunity to be found at the office—or right outside your own front door, for that matter. We're just being realistic enough to say that it isn't likely to march up to your door accompanied by a brass band and announce the chance of a lifetime.

Take the story of Tom Bata, head of the international Bata shoe company. When he was interviewed he often told a story he says his father used to relate: Two shoe salesmen were sent by the company to "open up" a poverty territory. Almost on arrival, one wired back: "Returning immediately! No one here wears shoes!" The other wired back: "Unlimited possibilities! Hardly anyone here wears shoes!"

Bata told this story often because the anecdote was in fact an excellent mirror of the philosophy of his company. Bata had manufacturing operations located all over the world. And all over the world, wherever his plane came down for a meeting or an inspection tour, the media were waiting to interview Tom Bata on how his success had been achieved. On one such tour cameras and reporters followed him from Sri Lanka to Bata's new million-dollar shoe-manufacturing plant in a remote and undeveloped area. When questioned about the wisdom of investing over a million dollars in such an unlikely place, Bata replied by relating his father's story concerning the two salesmen. His point was that opportunity is often what you make of circumstance—not necessarily what circumstance seems to offer. He went on to explain that his company had seen a double opportunity in what appeared to be a vast economic wasteland. His company wanted to develop a new market for an inexpensive shoe product and provide jobs for an impoverished people at the same time.

This leads us to four rules for conducting the search for opportunity:

1. *Emphasize viewpoint*. A positive point of view is part of the secret of snaring opportunity and thereby success. Viewpoint is certainly a good way to begin your approach to the business of opportunity.

   Many have observed the impact of viewpoint at work. George Bernard Shaw once commented, "People are always blaming their circumstances for what they are. I don't believe in circumstances. The people who get on in this world are the people who get up and look for the circumstances they want, and, if they can't find them, make them."

   Somewhere between the myth of waiting for opportunity to knock and Shaw's certainty that people who get on in the world get up and make the circumstances they want lies the natural question of "Yes, but *how?*" Is the answer really just a matter of viewpoint? Is it really just a matter of seeing an opportunity in a set of circumstances when others fail to see it? No. Viewpoint serves as a *spotlight on possibilities*, not an entire method for meeting opportunity face to face. So let's call viewpoint the first consideration of our four-point method of how to find and use opportunity.

2. *Take a chance on the possibilities.* Before spotlighting the second point, we'd like to ask you a few questions regarding some real people who rose from anonymity to achievement.

Would you bet on the future of this man? He is 53 years old. Most of his adult life has been a losing struggle against debt and misfortune. A war injury has denied him the use of his left hand. He has held several government jobs, succeeding at none, and he has often been in prison. Driven by personal motives and a willingness to make yet another effort to find his unknown future, he determines to write a book.

Would you hire a man with a deadpan face and an even deadlier monotone voice to be an on-camera television personality and produce the show? The man applying for the position is well aware of his apparent drawbacks, but he is determined to have the job.

Would you support this man for public office? He is a tailor's apprentice. History will show that he becomes, and remains, a tailor throughout his youth and young manhood. Destined never to attend formal school, he will be illiterate when he marries at 19, and finally it will be his wife who teaches him to read and write. He wants to do something important in life.

Would you believe this man, who says he has chosen to make music his career? He cannot read music, and he plunks the piano with two fingers. Music is all he thinks about.

Would you buy stock in the possibilities of these two women? They are housewives who have done nothing more businesslike for a number of years than raise families. Now some distance from their college educations and emotionally light-years from their early professional backgrounds, they have decided to undertake a venture that will place them in direct competition with some of the most aggressive and successful people in the business world. Under the circumstances even their husbands can offer little encouragement.

Did you guess the identities of any of these people?

The former prisoner wrote a book that has enthralled the world for more than 350 years: Cervantes called his book *Don Quixote*. The man with the monotone voice, the man so superficially ill suited for his chosen medium, both produced and starred in what became and remained the biggest show on television for nearly a quarter of a century: "The Ed Sullivan Show." The illiterate young tailor's apprentice became president of the United States: Andrew Johnson served as the seventeenth president of his country, from 1865 to 1869. The aspiring yet ill-prepared music man, Irving Berlin, gave the world a musical gift that will far outlast his lifetime. The two housewives founded a corporation and co-authored a book based on their teaching abilities and philosophies. As president and chairman of the board of their own corporation, they have taught courses and given seminars to thousands of people in the world of business, from Fortune 500 companies to international audiences on several continents. You are reading their book right now.

Did opportunity knock for these people? Not the way the world usually pictures it. In these instances several reasons—determination, ambition, desire, ability—all played a part. But the one reason for their success—the one most important thing these stories have in common—is *risk*. These people, and thousands upon thousands of others like them—and like you—were willing to reach out, to *risk the possibility of growth*—the possibility of success. They were willing to move forward in life and see what might come of it, to risk making an opportunity for themselves.

The second point, then, requires that you always be willing to consider the possibilities. Be willing to reach toward your unknown future, as Cervantes did. Be willing to risk personal growth, as Andrew Johnson and the authors of this book did. Be willing to make an opportunity out of nothing more than a possibility, as Ed Sullivan and Irving Berlin did.

3. *You have to pay your dues.* Hundreds of thousands of readers who had never heard of Erma Bombeck woke up to discover that a humorous column called "At Wit's End" had appeared in their hometown newspapers through the magic of syndication. Overnight, it seemed, Bombeck had "made it." She was 37 years old and a full-time homemaker in Ohio when it happened.

The interesting thing is that what actually happened began when Bombeck was in her early twenties. She was writing obituaries for the Dayton *Journal-Herald*, "and I couldn't get them right," she once told the *Saturday Evening Post*. That she was not a natural "factual" type destroyed her hopes of achieving her early goal of being a hard-nosed reporter in the trench-coat tradition. It necessitated a move to feature writing and a household-hints column. However, the newsroom lost her in her early twenties to marriage and family life, and it would be years before her husband would inadvertently trigger her "overnight" success by saying once too often, "Whatcha been doing all day?"

On just such a day in 1965, Erma Bombeck offered her idea for a column called "At Wit's

End" to the *Kettering-Oakwood Times* (in Ohio) for $3 per installment. National syndication followed within weeks.

Overnight? She began "paying her dues" and learning her craft when she started as a newspaper obituary writer. It only took another ten or fifteen years of life in the suburbs, discovering the right target at which to aim her talent, for her to become an overnight success.

A highly successful artist we overheard during an exhibition of her work removed forever the mythology of the overnight success with just two words. An admirer who had stood for some time in front of one of her paintings was moved to ask in appreciative awe, "How long did it take you to *do* that?"

"Forty years," she replied. "It takes a lifetime to blend emotion and sensitivity into the colors and brush strokes of a work of art."

You must pay your dues. Whether it be art, invention, writing, salesmanship, business acumen, politics, educational preparation for law or medicine or engineering—whatever your pursuit in life, you pay your dues to the association of experience. While it may not take you forty years, the artist's point is well taken: nothing is an overnight success, no matter what appearances may suggest.

When individuals or achievements are apparently thrust overnight from oblivion to the center stage of the world's attention, they have simply become more *visible* to us as an entire society. Network television and newspaper wire services—the grandest gossip system the world has ever known—gets wind of something interesting to millions of us simultaneously and instantly. But sudden visibility is *not* a synonym for overnight success. Don't be misled into believing that success just *happens* to other people and that it might *happen* to you the same way if only the opportunity would knock.

4. *Take action.* You *make* an opportunity out of a possiblity by initiating *one* move. One move at a time. Not a one-giant-step-into-the-spotlight kind of move, but much more often one small, unobtrusive move, which may draw little, if any, attention from the world at large.

Erma Bombeck saw the possibility. She had some funny views on life in the suburbs, and some people in Kettering, Ohio, had a newspaper. What about the possibility of getting together? She offered them her column. As moves go, that one went unreported. Millions of people did *not* read a headline saying OHIO HOUSEWIFE OFFERS COLUMN TO *KETTERING-OAKWOOD TIMES*!

The world did *not* knock at her door one morning and say, "Hey, we hear you're a very funny lady. Want to write a column for a few hundred newspapers and get rich and be famous? You know, TV and everything?"

"Woody Allen had a line I gobbled up once," Bombeck told the *Saturday Evening Post*. "He said if you're not failing, you're not trying anything. I read that and thought he was talking to me. He didn't mean we should go out and court failure, but that we need to take risks once in a while."

Thomas Edison, like so many others, risked it. Long before the media of his time discovered that he had invented the light bulb, he had been persisting in the notion that the opportunity to invent the light bulb was there. Time after time, through literally thousands of experiments, he tried to find the light and failed. Thomas Edison was among the millions of people in the world who failed their way to success one small, unobtrusive move at a time. Failure is one of opportunity's favorite disguises, it's good to remember.

"Ah, so," as the thoughtful Japanese say, there *is* a how-to, a businesslike method of approaching opportunity. We don't need to be taken in by any flirta tious hit-or-miss philosophy. Before we review the four points of the method, we'd like to give you our list of *don't*s:

> *Don't wait for opportunity to knock*. The business of opportunity is not romantic fiction, it's a very organized business of perspective and action.
>
> *Don't wait for something for nothing* to land in your lap, for your luck to turn, your ship to come in, for overnight success. Put those myths to rest and get on with your business.
>
> *Don't wait for one big chance of a lifetime*. Waiting is the major activity of that idea. Using opportunity is a business of one *small* chance at a time.
>
> *Don't wait for circumstances to change*. Do something now!

Do make one move, no matter how small or unobtrusive it may seem in the total scheme of things. It makes no difference at all if anyone else takes notice at this point. This move's for *you*. United Press International and NBC and all the gang can catch up with you on the next one. Your *first* move may have been choosing to read this book, a move toward learning to speak the language of success. While you have all this in mind, consider the possibilities. Give some thought to what you might like to do next—and review the method:

Four-Point Method for Meeting Opportunity Face to Face

1. *Emphasize viewpoint*. It spotlights possibility for you. Keep a positive attitude and have an open mind.
2. *Take a chance*. Be willing to risk, to reach out and take hold of a possibility. Learn that success is never certain; failure is never final.
3. *Pay your dues*. They buy you the knowledge

and experience to accept possibility's challenging ideas and risks. While you're considering all the possibilities, go about the daily business of paying your dues to the association of experience.

4. *Take action*. It stimulates change, moves circumstances and *makes* opportunity out of possibility, one step at a time. You don't have to leap tall buildings in a single bound to become successful.

It seems that all those anonymous voices and those we know by name, like Bernard Shaw, were right when they said, *You make your own opportunity*. It not only *can* be done, *anyone* can do it.

And by the time you have finished this book, we hope you will see how you can do it, too, because you will have applied the four concepts—*opportunity, organized listening, prepared communication* and *controlled assets*—to the possibilities that you have in mind for yourself.

Opportunity is the first of our four concepts because so much is built on it, verbally and practically speaking, but we began with it for one other reason. We wanted you to have a clear perspective on both the outdated myths and the objective methods of opportunity.

Now, with that in mind, you should be ready to consider the next concept in learning to speak the language of success: *organized listening*.

· 2 ·
Organized Listening
(Listen Before You Leap)

On his first day back at work after his vacation, Guy was joined at the coffee break by Perry, who worked in another department.

"Hey, Guy, how was the vacation?" Perry greeted him. "Looks like it couldn't have been too bad because you sure have a great tan."

"Well, the weather in the Bahamas is beautiful," Guy said. "And I really enjoyed all the water sports. They have these boats they call catamarans—"

"I've always like water sports myself," Perry interrupted. "The only trouble is that I can't take a lot of sun, like some people." He smiled. "Man, I really envy that tan. I just get red. Oh, by the way, I've been meaning to ask you how your talk to your Rotary Club went."

"It went quite well," Guy said. "And I got to talk to some very interesting people about their plans for an open-space school that—"

"Somebody's always coming up with some harebrained new idea in education," Perry said. "What they should do is forget the fancy stuff and get back to basics. Did you have a chance to do any fishing on your vacation?"

"Yes, as a matter of fact I did get to do some deep-sea fishing," Guy said, smiling as he recalled it. "I caught the biggest marlin that anyone ever—"

"Last time I went deep-sea fishing was back in '76 on a charter off the Florida coast," Perry interrupted again. "You know, you just can't beat the thrill of fighting one of those sailfish. There's nothing like it. Ever catch a sailfish?"

"No," Guy said. "Only a marlin."

"Oh. Anything new happening in your department?" Perry asked.

"We have a new government contract that—"

"Watch out. Those government contracts can be murder," Perry said. "The paperwork can nickel and dime away all your profit if you're not careful. Have you done your scheduling yet? We had a government contract two years ago and nearly lost our shirts on it because we staffed early and then the government didn't adhere to the schedule."

"I have to go," Guy said; then he stood up and walked away. Perry looked around, spotted Glen and Fenton at another table and took his cup of coffee over there.

"What's new, fellas?" he said as he interrupted their conversation. "I was just talking to Guy, but he didn't seem to be in a very good mood. What do you suppose is bothering him?"

Glen and Fenton didn't have to answer Perry's question about what they thought was bothering Guy. Perry was already talking about something else, and they were getting ready to walk away, too.

So many budding conversations, before they have a chance to bloom, are squashed by people who talk too much because they think that communicating means "listen to *me*." There are more conversations brought to full flower by good *listeners* than there are by good *talkers*.

The truly good listener is a rare and precious person,

a treasure to everyone who ever has had something to say. All of us want to know that when we talk, somebody out there is listening.

If you've ever been talking to someone and suddenly had the very uncomfortable feeling that you had completely lost his attention—or never had it from the beginning—you were probably reluctant to ask, "Are you listening to me?" No one likes to feel that he is wasting his words. Everyone wants to communicate with a person who listens and lets you know that he is listening and understanding and thinking about what you are saying.

Why then are there fewer good listeners than there are good talkers? One reason might be that we generally place more emphasis on developing the skills of conversation from the talking point of view than we do from the listening point of view. And another reason could be that it actually is easier to talk than to listen.

According to researchers, it is harder for us to listen than to talk because we actually can listen faster than we can speak. The speed of our speech is about 125 words a minute, but our thinking processes occur at least four times faster than that. In other words, in the same amount of time that it takes the other person to say 100 words to you, you have the capacity to listen to 400. It's apparent that that leaves a whole lot of spare time for thinking, and that is where the trouble begins.

What often happens is that while someone is talking, the mind of the undisciplined listener begins to leave the speaker, then dart back, leave and dart back, again and again, until that one time when it stays away a little bit too long. Then it returns, only to find that the speaker is too far ahead and part of what he said has been missed.

It often happens just like this: He and she are approaching each other on the street. She sees him first and wishes she hadn't run into him, because he's so dull. She briefly considers ducking into a doorway until he's passed, but it's too late. There is no escape, for he has already seen her and greeted her.

As she returns his greeting, she thinks: Boy, what

rotten luck! If I'd had any idea that I was going to run into him today, I would have stayed home. Let's see, what excuse can I use to get away?

Meanwhile he has been talking to her, and now she hears him say, ". . . the biggest break of my career. I'm really looking forward to setting up the overseas field office in Paris."

She says, "What? What was that you said about going to France?"

"Oh, nothing," he says and shrugs. "Well, see you around." As he walks away he thinks, I wish I hadn't bothered to stop to talk to her. She wasn't at all interested that I've been made vice-president in charge of overseas business. And to think I almost asked her if she'd like to apply for the job as my assistant. If I ever see her again, I'll head the other way.

The unlucky lady's problem is that she listens to herself more than she does to others. By not giving her full attention to others when they are speaking, she is shirking her share of the responsibility for what happens between them. It's too bad that she doesn't realize that communication needs a listener as much as it does a speaker. Without a listener, a speaker is just creating sound.

It's too bad she hasn't learned how to take control and organize her listening. As an organized listener, she would have been using that spare time to ask herself what she was hearing and how she understood what was being said. She would have known how to keep her own thoughts and feelings separate from her listening, and she would have been able to concentrate and listen without distraction. Keeping her mind alert and her curiosity healthy would help her listen more actively and continue to develop better habits of listening.

If it seems that there is a lot involved in becoming an organized listener, that's because there really is. Good listening is not a passive activity. It is hard mental work, and it requires self-discipline. But it can become a labor of love for the person who really cares about other people.

People must talk to other people. Talking helps us solve problems, create new ideas, and discover new directions; helps us be less isolated, less frightened and less alone; helps us feel more appreciated, more worthy and more significant. And it is the *listener* who makes all that possible.

Good listening is a very powerful aspect of effective communicating, and yet good listeners are so rare that being really listened to by someone who can tell you what *you said* rather than what *he thinks* is an exceptional experience. A good listener should be able to give feedback that, figuratively, takes the words right out of the speaker's mouth. That person knows that you are really listening to him, and he will become more involved and more enthusiastic and more ready to return the favor.

Once you have learned how to organize your own listening, you will find it much easier and much more exciting to listen to others. Because the more and the better you listen—and the more you comprehend of what others are saying—the clearer and deeper your understanding of others—and of yourself—becomes. It's always a pleasant feeling when you can do something for others at the same time that you help yourself.

But before you can begin to do all that, you have to put yourself in a mood to want to listen. You have to be willing, first of all, to make your personal commitment to *organized listening*.

Organized listening requires a commitment because it means more than just letting sound waves enter your ears. It means that you must be an alert and active participant in the process. It means overcoming poor listening habits—such as hearing only what you expect or want to hear, or being easily distracted—that interfere with good listening. It means beginning to hear other people less from inside yourself, less from your preconceptions of them, and being willing to know them and accept them more as they actually are. That is what the concepts of organized listening are based on, and we recommend them to anyone who wants to become a more effective communicator.

Organized listening may be a totally new idea to you. The chances are good that you never even thought there could be such a thing. You always thought that listening came naturally, like ears. But if you are the kind of person who is willing to consider a new approach, then we believe you can begin to take control and be a more effective communicator by using some of the concepts of organized listening every day. You can start right now.

We don't think you'll ever regret it. If you are willing to try something new, if you are willing to organize your listening habits for maximum effectiveness, if you are willing to make organized listening an expression of your genuine interest in others and of your desire to be more successful with others, a very pleasant experience is ahead.

Before you begin your journey into organized listening, read the story that follows and do the accompanying exercise.

> Jackie and two boyfriends were jogging down a country road. They passed a house. A couple was having an argument. Pieces of pottery were scattered around the floor. The telephone rang three times. A neighbor was concerned about his friends.

After reading this story, read the following six statements *without looking back at the story* and classify them as *true, false* or *need more information*.

	True	False	Need More Information
1. Three boys were jogging down a country road.			
2. They looked in a window and saw people arguing.			
3. A husband and wife were having an argument.			
4. Broken pieces of pottery were scattered around the floor.			
5. The telephone rang three times.			
6. A neighbor was on the phone.			

The story you read and the statements you evaluated are an exercise in listening that we use in our seminars. What we try to demonstrate with it is that no matter how they listen, people tend to see things through their own mental windows.

For example, people who know a person named Jackie who happens to be a female usually thinks immediately that the first statement is false. People who know a person named Jackie who is a male generally think that this statement is true. People who are aware that Jackie can be either a masculine or a feminine name say that they need more information.

The same thing happens with the other statements. The story does not specify that anyone looked in a window, but some people interpret it to mean that Jackie and friends had to look into the house to see the couple arguing. Other people realize that they may have been on the front porch or that someone might have looked in the door. Again, you need more information. The word *couple* to some people always means "man and wife." To others it can mean two men or two women or an unmarried man and woman. So, again, you need more information. Some people assume that the pottery was broken because it is in scattered pieces. Others are aware that a piece need not be broken but may merely be a divided part, such as a piece out of a set of china or a piece of bread. A potter creates a "piece" of pottery, which is whole. The statement "the telephone rang three times" is true. That a neighbor was concerned about his friends does not necessarily mean that the neighbor was on the phone. He or she could have been in the house or sitting on the sofa next to the phone. You need more information.

Different people have different interpretations of these statements. The interpretations are usually as varied as the people themselves and their experiences.

That is why in business five people can go to the same meeting and hear something different. They all go to the meeting with different backgrounds and with different perceptions, wanting to hear different things. They sit through it unconsciously disregarding everything that is said that does not fit what they want or expect to hear. That's what makes it so difficult for people to be good listeners.

The average person absorbs only thirty percent of what he or she hears and, a week later, has retained only ten percent. Learning to organize your listening—knowing what you want to listen for—gives you more control. You can increase what you comprehend beyond that average thirty-percent limitation.

· 3 ·
Learn the
Other Person's Name
(The Name Is the Game)

Without ever having met you personally, we can describe the most interesting, charming, warm, polite and successful person *you* ever met in just six words: *the one who remembered your name*. The reason we're so sure of ourselves is that we're all human, and it's human nature to feel innately complimented and respected by the person who remembers our name. This is because our own name is such an important part of our personal identity and sense of self-worth.

The first rule in the art of listening for social and business success is to remember names. The point bears reiterating. *Listen for names and repeat them.*

Remembering someone's name is the easiest way to win with words, to open closed doors, to reach people who are hard to get through to on the phone and generally to succeed in business without really trying (or seeming to, at least).

"Good morning, Ms. . . . ?" said the saleswoman, offering her hand in such a straightforward, friendly manner that it would have been impossible for the secretary not to finish the introduction.

". . . James, Mrs. James," she replied, finishing the sentence as they shook hands. "May I help you?"

"Yes, I'm sure you can, Mrs. James," the young woman said pleasantly, repeating the secretary's name. "I've just taken over this territory for the Hubbard Company, and I'm making a special effort to meet all the company's customers personally. I realize I don't have an appointment this morning, but if you could ask Mr. Allen to spare me a moment while I'm here, I assure you I won't stay long enough to throw his schedule off."

Take a look at all the right things this young saleswoman did, beginning with listening for the name she needed and then reinforcing the importance of that name by *repeating* it. She then went on to make Mrs. James her ally by the use of the phrase "yes, you *can* (help me)," which put a subtle responsibility on Mrs. James to follow through with her offer of assistance. The saleswoman further enlisted Mrs. James in her foot-in-the-door campaign by using the words *special effort* and *personally* in describing her need to see Mr. Allen. Her final two clinchers: "if *you* could ask" him to spare *me* a moment (making it a personal favor somehow offered and accepted between the two of them); the personal wording of "I assure *you*" in her promise not to stay long got Mrs. James off the emotional hook of whether or not to interrupt her boss with an unscheduled caller.

We're betting she got in. And more than that, we're betting she started off with "Mr. Allen, how nice to meet you. I appreciate these few minutes for us to get acquainted," while she was shaking his hand. Knowing how well it worked, she wouldn't have missed the chance to repeat his name. Her use of the phrase "for *us* to get acquainted" automatically personalized the moment, removing any sense of an adversary salesman-versus-buyer relationship, comfortably changing it to a feeling of "our chance" to visit together.

Contrast our mythical saleswoman's success with the experience of our friend Al, who's still kicking himself over the name game. Al is a boating enthusiast. While he was at the airport, he ran into a casual acquaintance he'd met at the lake and visited with him for about thirty minutes. The man said he was very eager to buy a boat just like Al's. As a matter of fact, would Al consider selling? No, Al was very happy with his boat. However, a week later Al was told he was being transferred. Now he wanted to sell his boat, but he couldn't remember the name of the man who wanted to buy it. If he'd been listening—*really* listening—in that conversation—not just paying mock attention for the sake of minimal courtesy—he wouldn't have had to sell his boat at a loss.

But the prize for one-hundred-percent effort in listening for names goes to the president of a large company, who scored a personal and permanent success with one of his firm's employees. The two had been introduced briefly in a company planning meeting several months before. As they were about to pass each other in the hall, the president unexpectedly nodded and said, "Hello, Tom. Everything going all right in your department?"

Out of the several hundred people the company employed, the president had taken the time to listen attentively for Tom's full name on the only occasion they had met. Noting that Tom was a very tall and big man, he had used a simple name association to remind himself that the head of his materials purchasing department was tall and seemed easily big enough to cover a lot of ground. He had no trouble recalling Tall Tom Acre's name when he wanted to personalize his greeting with the respect of a name remembered. Over many years Tom never forgot the attention.

Being made to feel as valuable as we are in business or personal settings of any kind is the best verbal communication. Listening for names, making name associations with images you can recall easily and repeating people's names are three ways to improve your success in almost any situation: three parts of one basic skill. But keep in mind that listening comes first. If you don't *hear* a name you can neither associate it nor repeat it. Listening for names is the first name of the game of winning with words.

· 4 ·
Listening for Filing
Purposes (A Good File
Opens Many a Door)

An old Indian had earned a reputation for having a flawless memory. It was said that he never forgot a face or name and that he was able to recall at will the most minute details.

The devil, hearing of the old man's reputation, offered him a challenge. Maintaining that there was no such thing as a perfect memory, the devil dared the chief to agree to forfeit his soul if the old Indian ever forgot anything. The chief confidently accepted the wager.

Then the devil asked, "Do you like eggs?" The Indian replied "Yes," and the devil went away.

Twenty years later the chief died, and the devil thought, Now here's my chance to take his soul. He came back to earth and confronted the old Indian. Raising his hand in the tribal salutation, the devil said, "How."

The old Indian replied, "Fried."

The devil lost his bet and his option on the chief's soul. The story isn't true, but it makes a valid point: you never know when you might hear something that could be of tremendous value to you or to your company.

Every day great opportunities are lost because not everyone realizes the potential value of some of the information he or she hears. Most of us spend much of our time listening *to* information but have not learned how to attune the mind to listening *for* it. As a result, we don't always recognize what we hear as something we should *file away*. Then when we need that information, perhaps two months later, it is lost. We didn't keep it available. We didn't secure it while we had the opportunity.

Have you ever had an experience like John D.'s? Beginning a well-earned trip to the Bahamas, John introduced himself to Ann E., his seatmate on the airplane.

During the course of the conversation, Ann said, "I'm on a business trip for my company, Quantum Constituent Components. They're sending me to a seminar to learn some ways that other firms are using to deal with turnover problems. We had a terribly high rate this past year. We lost some of our key people."

"That's always a serious problem," John sympathized. "I hope you get the information you need from the seminar."

At the airport the two passengers separated, transferring to different flights. John spent his two weeks in the sun and returned to his desk at Prosper and Boon Ameliorations, Ltd., refreshed and eager to get back to work. Sorting through the mail that had accumulated while he was away, John came upon the latest in-house memo. The memo was from the training department, and it highlighted ways to reduce high employee turnover.

Recalling his in-flight conversation with Ann, John made a call to the Training Programs Department of Prosper and Boon and said, "Quantum Constituent is having a turnover problem. Maybe you ought to call them and suggest setting up some courses there to help people relate better to each other."

Then he called the Benefits Programs Department and suggested they also call Quantum to see if they might be interested in giving their employees more benefits. John gave the name of Ann E. to both department heads as a person with whom to establish contact at Quantum.

Following up on John's information, they made the sales. John's ability to demonstrate his interest in all facets of his company's operations was appreciated and helped him move ahead.

More and more executives we talk to say that they place a high value on those employees who *listen* for and take note of anything that might be of any assistance to the company—and then let the company know.

You probably know people like John, who seem to have an aptitude for remembering information that, although it is seemingly insignificant when first heard, acquires importance with the passing of time. It might be something about a new company moving into the area, which could be a supplier for their company; or somebody met professionally or socially who mentioned a new way to deal with customers; or perhaps a new motivational idea.

It takes no special capacity to *listen for filing purposes*. You never know when you might hear something that could be of importance to your company. When you go to a convention where you are dealing with people professionally and socially, making contacts, talking with them, you may hear of a new procedure that has been developed or tried successfully. With so many of us working in fields that have rapid rates of obsolescence, it becomes especially important to listen tor filing purposes.

A technique we have found successful is to pretend that you have a treasure chest in your brain and that every person you meet has a gem of knowledge to add to that chest. You may on occasion find yourself listening to someone who seems to be a total bore. You wonder if you should keep on conversing with him or move to the other side of the room. But if you haven't gotten your gem of information, keep talking to him. Maybe the other person isn't really listening to you. Maybe the other person seems only self-interested. But stay in there! Too many people simply don't hang on long enough to succeed. Almost everyone will give you something good if you'll only be persistent. But you can't turn it on and off, and you have got to believe that you can get a gem from everybody. It may be that there are some people you simply cannot get a gem from, and you may finally have to give up after having made a sincere, genuine effort. But the more you *listen for filing purposes*, the more the odds will be in your favor. And the more you will find yourself experiencing that wonderful feeling when, six months or a year later, you can take out a gem and use it.

There's also a fringe benefit to listening for filing purposes. As you become more adept at staying in there with everyone and not tuning out, you will become a better conversationalist. When you automatically say to yourself, "I'm listening for filing purposes," you'll begin to listen wisely and well, even when it occasionally becomes very difficult.

It's worth the effort. As Wilson Mizner said, "A good listener is not only popular everywhere, but after a while he gets to know something."

· 5 ·
Listen to Give Information
(Be Well Read
—Well Ahead)

Two men were having a conversation in the elevator of
the office building in which they worked.

"Have you ever gotten a letter that brought back
vivid memories of the past?" the first man asked, smiling happily.

"Have I ever?" the second man said with a look of
misery on his face. "I just got one from the IRS remind-
ing me that I owe them two thousand dollars plus interest from three years ago!"

That's the nature of memory. Left to its own devices,
it is highly selective, recalling pleasant things and forgetting the unpleasant things, at least until they are forced
into our consciousness by something like a reminder
from the IRS. But you can make use of that to improve
your memory for details. Through *association* you can
lock in details and keep them at your beck and call. It
requires only some organization of your thinking: to
listen for the opening in a conversation, and when the
time is right, to give information that you just happen to
possess.

Why should you bother learning how to listen to give

information? Because when information comes to you from many different sources, you remember that you received it but aren't able to call it back when you need it. You may miss many opportunities because of that inability to master information.

In the social and business worlds, listening to give information means being *prepared* to begin and carry on conversations. Many times we find ourselves with dead silence between us and the other person, and it is a terribly helpless feeling. Haven't you ever found yourself standing next to someone important to your career or social standing, perhaps the president of your company, and begun thinking desperately, Oh, please let me think of something interesting to say!

Have you ever read something in a newspaper or magazine, then been at a party where people started talking about that very thing and you could remember reading about it but not *what* you read? You just stood there unhappily asking yourself, "What *was* it that I read about this subject?" You've lost a terrific opportunity to join in, to contribute something, to make a good impression and to socialize. What makes it even worse is having the information you were struggling so hard to call up pop into your mind in full detail the morning *after* the party.

Haven't you also been in a situation where there has been a silence, and yet someone was able to start and carry on a conversation? You've often heard people say, "Funny you should mention that. Just last week I read the most interesting article about it."

The difference between you and the other people was that they had probably *prepared* and *planned* and *listened to give* the information at just the right time.

There's a way you can be sure that the next time you're part of a group, either business or social, and they start having an interesting discussion about some topic of special interest, you can participate with confidence.

Let's start with a technique we call *directed reading*. We believe that if you keep in mind the idea of talking about what you are reading, you will retain more of it. Form a mental image as you read an article. Visualize the particular person or group with whom you will share it verbally. Visualize yourself talking to that person or group; as you read, you will make a pleasant mental association that will stay with you.

Tom J. was comptroller for a soap manufacturing firm. He read an article that had some interesting ideas for advertising soap products. Tom saved the article, putting it away in a file he kept for this purpose.

Six months later Tom was asked to attend a convention. Before he left for the convention, he remembered the article, took it from his file and read it again. When he arrived at the convention, he listened for some of the executives to start talking about advertising, and then he brought forth the information he had gotten from the article, contributing to the discussion and probably furthering his career.

He had read something, knew he was going to use it again and *filed it away*. When the opportunity came, he remembered it, refreshed himself on the information and used it.

It is important to have a filing system. Top executives all over the country tell us that they keep filing cabinets filled with all kinds of information. Then, during the course of their usual business and social activities, they *listen to give that information*.

All of us meet people and learn a lot about them, but because our memories aren't perfectly reliable, we can't be sure we will be able to recall what we learned the next time we meet them. Keeping a file on people you meet can make you a popular person as well as one admired for your memory. It takes only a little discipline.

When you are meeting someone new, listen for all the information he gives you about himself. When you get back to your office or home, make a file card, writing on it the person's name and everything you learned about him, such as that he is about to make a trip to Canada, has two children and his hobby is flying model airplanes. The next time you know you are going to see that person, you won't have to depend completely on your fallible memory. You can take out that card beforehand, look it over and then *listen for an opportunity* to ask about the trip to Canada, or the children, or his hobby. He will admire your wonderful memory. He will be so pleased that you remembered so much about him that he may never forget about you.

While you are reading a newspaper or magazine, stay alert for things that interest the people you know. For example, you might happen to see an article or a news item about a certain football team not doing well this season. You know that one of your associates is really gung ho on football. She knows everything about the teams and the players and their standings in the NFL. During football season that's all she wants to discuss. When you read this article or news item, say to yourself, "Aha! Georgia loves football, it's football season and I'm having dinner with her Tuesday night. I'm going to remember to talk to her about this coach and this team. I don't know much about football, but I'm going to ask Georgia why she thinks this coach is having problems."

Then *visualize* Georgia, and visualize yourself talking to her at dinner. Imagine how you're going to bring up the subject and phrase the question. *Visualize* how pleased Georgia will be and how well the conversation will go. All that will make the article more interesting to you, too. You'll probably find yourself impatient for Tuesday night because you know you're going to be able to talk to Georgia about football.

This technique will work with any friend or associate, in any field of interest. If your friend Larry is in the housing construction business, every time you see some interesting news about that industry you'll pay attention because you know that when you see Larry, you will have something to talk to him about. If your friend Sue is an office manager and you find an article about the latest developments in word processors, you will look forward to seeing Sue so that you can talk to her about what you've learned. If your employer's wife collects antique automobiles and you read an article about that, you will not find yourself standing dumbly beside her at the office Christmas party, praying for an inspiration to fall from heaven and land on you. You will be prepared to talk about what you've learned about antique automobiles. And that's important, too—*you* are also learning. So find the information, file it away and then listen for opportunities to use it.

When you give a dinner party, you go to a lot of trouble to serve gourmet specialties and have fresh flowers in the centerpiece. You use your best china and heirloom silver and have the house looking like a magazine photograph. But how many times do you go to that much trouble to make sure the conversation flows? And yet what is it that makes a dinner party—or any social gathering—truly memorable? It's the conversation, of course. We remember the table talk long after we've forgotten what was on the menu.

Often you're fortunate and the conversation just flows naturally. Usually it's because you have the right combination of people together at the right time, and so it just works perfectly. But every once in a while it doesn't flow at all. You can and should be prepared for that eventuality with some bons mots to throw out to stimulate the conversation.

An effective way to utilize an interesting bit of information is just to present the information and, reserving your own opinion, phrase a question around it. This device is illustrated by a dinner party Franklin S. was invited to, at which none of the guests knew each other very well. They sat down to dinner and just looked at each other uncomfortably.

Franklin said to them, "We had an interesting discussion at lunch today. We discussed which word is more emotion packed, *aggressive* or *assertive*." Then he asked, "If someone were to say to you that you were aggressive or assertive, which one would you take as a compliment and why?" Everyone had a different view of these two words, so everybody got into the conversation. They spent a whole hour at dinner just talking about those words, the difference between them, especially as related to men and women, and how different words have different meanings for people.

The ice was broken, and the conversation, once started, continued to flow nicely after that. Franklin had *filed away some information* and then had *listened for an opportunity to use it.*

There are many similar techniques you can depend on to get a group of strangers talking enthusiastically. File them away and then listen for an opportunity to throw them into the conversational arena.

When you know that you are going to be with a group of people and will be expected to make conversation, think beforehand about what you could talk about if no one else seems to be prepared. There are any number of interesting items in the newspaper every day. While you're reading, look for things that would be interesting for everyone in the group to discuss. Make mental notes of the details, using the imagery technique so that they are implanted in your memory. Maybe you won't need to use them because the conversation won't require any assistance or stimulation, but you will be ready should you have to lend a helping word. Then you only need tell the story, and throw in your own comments if you choose, and soon everybody will be involved in the who, what, where, when and how of it. Even if no solutions come out of it, you will all have an interesting time because you were prepared beforehand and listened for an opportunity to give information.

The technique of *listening to give information* has a very important application to business meetings. Have you ever gone to a meeting and walked out afterward furious with yourself because you had forgotten to say what you wanted to say? Or did you ever say to yourself, ''Well, I meant to, but I just didn't think about it at the time''? There are two possible explanations for that happening. One is that you were prepared but you just didn't get the right moment to speak; the other is that you just weren't prepared.

Many times you go into a business meeting with several points you want to make or ideas you want to propose. Knowing human nature for what it is, you expect somebody to knock down two or three of the things you present. You know you are not going to get everything you want; you never do. But there is a way by which you have an excellent chance of getting all your ideas or proposals before the group. This technique is called *coat-tailing*.

What we mean by *coat-tailing* is listening for somebody to give you something—a statement or even just one word—on which you can elaborate. Then grab that coat-tail, express your support of the person who said it and use it to lead into what you want to say.

The problem for most people walking into a meeting with six proposals is that they are so intent on getting their proposals out that they don't listen to anyone else. They just throw in their ideas without first winning some allies.

But if you're *listening to give information,* and listening very carefully, you can coat-tail, amplify on another person's idea or word and win his support for your own idea. Communication works on this principle: if you support the other person, he will want to support you. The more allies you can win, the more receptive the other people will be to your ideas.

For example, if Allen says, "I think we should have a mail campaign to promote the opening of our new store," and you've been wanting a mail campaign using introductory discount cards, you can say: "Allen is right. A mail campaign is an excellent idea. We need to promote the new store, and that's the way to do it. And perhaps we should enclose discount cards for opening day."

You have *amplified* on what Allen said, just as though it was Allen who inspired you to think of mailing out discount cards. By coat-tailing your idea to Allen's, you've been able to introduce one of your ideas, you have shown Allen that you really support his idea and you have probably won his support for your proposal, too. That accomplished, you can now listen to everyone else, waiting again to hear something onto which you can coat-tail another of your ideas. Wait for the right words, the right time, a suitable pause, and say, "You know, what Randy has brought up is important and I agree with him. Now I'd like to bring up this point."

Now you have a much better chance of getting all your ideas adopted than if you had just tossed them out and hoped for the best.

We cannot stress too much the importance of being *prepared* with what you want to say. Being prepared requires a great deal of attention. That means you have a presentation ready, even if it lasts no more than thirty seconds and may not seem like a presentation to anyone else. The point is that you will be prepared with it.

You will have prepared yourself by using *directed reading,* consciously planning to be able to talk about what you have read. You will have prepared yourself by *keeping a file,* referring to it when you know a person you're going to be with will be interested in a certain subject. You will have prepared and planned carefully so that you can at least ask a good question.

You will be prepared to *listen to give information.*

Preparation and planning are the foundation on which the successful use of listening to give information is built.

• 6 •

Don't Be Distracted by
Emotion-Packed Words
(Verbal Hot Tamales)

Mary A. arrived at work on time as usual on Monday morning, and as was her habit, she pleasantly greeted each of her co-workers as she passed them on the way to her desk. Mary thoroughly enjoyed her job with Rosebud Ladies Wear, Inc., and was an enthusiastic worker who felt she could look forward to a secure future with the company.

But on this particular day, just as Mary turned her attention to the work before her, her boss burst into the room with some invoice sheets clutched in his hand and angrily demanded, "Mary, how could you do this?"

Mary was visibly, and understandably, upset by the accusatory tone of her boss's question and voice. She could tell she was being blamed for something even though at this point she had no idea what it was she was supposed to have done.

"How could you do this?" her boss repeated, angered even more by Mary's silence.

Thoroughly intimidated, Mary somehow managed to respond, inquiring in a timid voice, "What did I do?"

"You know what you did!" her boss shouted. "You ordered five hundred more of those seersucker wrap-arounds. How could you be so stupid?"

Feeling now that she had been attacked by being called stupid, Mary attempted to defend herself. "Well, that's what you said I should do!" she countered indignantly.

"Why would I have said that when I know we already have that many in inventory?" her boss insisted.

"But I'm sure you told me the other day . . . that is, I counted . . . I wouldn't make a mistake like that!" Mary stammered, getting all caught up in a lot of words. Mary's boss, totally frustrated and infuriated by Mary's defensiveness and inarticulateness, stormed out. For the rest of the day, Mary dabbed at her teary eyes with a crumpled tissue as she tried to justify herself to herself and her co-workers by muttering things like, "I can never do anything right. . . . Nobody around here ever tells me anything. . . . It's his fault for not making it clear."

Poor Mary! Not only was she too upset to work at her usual high level of performance, but she knew that her relationship with her boss and the course of her future with Rosebud Ladies Wear, Inc., had been irreparably damaged.

And what of Mary's boss? He was made only too painfully aware of the damage done to Mary's ability to function after their strained encounter, when the work he was depending on Mary to produce didn't flow across his desk as usual. He shouldn't have been too surprised to find on his desk the next morning, instead of Mary's usual folio of productivity, a neatly typed letter of resignation. Mary now felt so estranged from her boss that she felt obliged to quit because "there's no way I can please him." She was trapped.

She left Rosebud, Inc., even though she had really enjoyed working there and had planned to stay on, contributing her talents for many more years.

Mary's boss, a loyal Rosebud, Inc., employee for

whom Mary had once worked very well, was in the untenable position of either apologizing or accepting Mary's resignation, neither of which he really wanted to do. He was also trapped.

If this sort of thing is repeated too often, the company will lose other good employees—probably including Mary's boss. And all because two people reacted badly.

All Mary wanted was to be able to take pride in her work, to carry out her responsibilities to the company and to satisfy her boss's expectations of her. Mary's boss actually wanted the same things Mary did, for Mary and for himself, too. But neither got what he or she wanted, and nobody even knew why. What they were not consciously aware of was that while their *feelings* were reasonable, their *reactions* were wrong. They didn't understand that just because you feel attacked doesn't mean you have to attack back. And so, as in the nursery rhyme about a kingdom being lost for want of a horseshoe nail, the "ripple effect" spread out to become an engulfing wave over which they had no control. They didn't know they had an alternative.

If we could give Mary what she probably lay awake all night wishing for, we would take her back in time and give her the "nail" she needed to save the situation and create the ending she wanted. We think the scenario could have gone more like this:

Mary's boss burst into the room and angrily demanded, "Mary, how could you do this?"

Mary recognized the accusatory tone of her boss's question and voice and, understandably, she didn't like it. She could tell she was being blamed for something even though at this point she had no idea what it was.

"This is emotion-packed," she said to herself. Then in a calm voice she asked her boss, "What's the problem?"

Her boss, somewhat mollified by Mary's manner, replied less angrily, "The problem is that you ordered more of those seersucker wraparounds than I wanted you to order."

Mary studied the invoices her boss had tossed on her desk and said, "I think there may be some misunderstanding here. When we talked last week, it looked as though we needed this many. But I could have miscounted."

Instead of attacking back, Mary was thinking rationally: The problem is that he thinks I ordered too many. Why did I order that many? Why did I do what I did? Did I do it? Did I make a mistake, or did I do it because there was a good reason to do it? With her thinking organized, Mary was able to explain everything to her boss's satisfaction. Now Mary and her boss were carrying on a conversation instead of having a conflict. They were dealing with the issue, not the emotion, and Mary was no longer simply reacting badly. As a result of Mary's skill at controlling the situation, her career benefited and she continued to enjoy her boss's esteem as well as a reputation for being a dependable employee. As long as Mary keeps *listening not to be distracted by emotion-packed words*, she won't have to react to her feelings of being under siege. She won't have to yell back, and the one who doesn't yell ultimately gets the control.

Of course, Mary's boss also was very wrong in using emotion-packed words and in raising his voice, because these certainly don't bring out the best in anyone. But he was probably unaware of the ways in which he used them, as are most people. It's so easy to put others on the defensive, but the moment you have someone on the defensive, you are unable to communicate. A manager who thoughtlessly calls an employee's input a stupid idea can create an unspoken or a delayed reaction in the employee. That person may think, I'm not doing my job well, or he doesn't think much of me. At the least he will hesitate to offer his opinions or ideas again; at the worst he will start looking for another job. Either way the company and the manager may be losing out on some valuable talents and services because communication has been cut off by a careless remark.

What happened between Mary and her boss happens

in business all the time, but it is basically no different from what we see and hear happening, for example, between parents and children.

It's much nicer for parents to be able to say to their children that they are unselfish, kind and considerate, and of course parents want their children to think of them as thoughtful, understanding and generous. No parent wakes up in the morning determined to give his kids a hard time, and kids don't really deliberately set out to drive their parents mad. So why does it always end up with the kids being mean and stubborn and the parent yelling and screaming? Probably because so often the kids throw those emotion-packed words at the parents, and Mom and Dad react too quickly, without taking time to think, and get themselves caught in a bind in which they've *got* to be angry at the kids. You know what some of those emotion-packed words are because you have probably used them yourself. Remember "You're so *old-fashioned!*" And "When *I* have kids I'll be good to them." Or "I'm the only kid on the block who doesn't have his own car, and *it's your fault!*"

Sometimes Mom and Dad, reacting badly to juvenile behavior, issue arbitrary commands like "You clean up your room right now, *or else!*" Then they're really caught, because after yelling and screaming without effect, as usual, they've got to be angry at Junior because he still hasn't done what they wanted him to do.

The same thing happens in business. People throw those emotion-packed words at you, probably without realizing what they're doing, and you lose your temper and say things for which you will probably have to apologize later. We do not mean to say that you should never get angry; that would be an impossible dictum, anyway. You're a human being, and human beings get angry. It's an inalienable right, as well as part of your human nature. What we do mean to say is that you should get angry because you have *decided* to get angry, not because someone has *made* you angry.

You frequently hear children complain, "I couldn't

help it. He made me angry.'' But children have very little control over what they do with their feelings. As an adult, you don't have to let anyone *make* you angry, certainly not against your will. You have that control; you don't have to give it to anyone else.

Who hasn't had to deal with a salesperson who is just being rude and surly? Have you ever lost your temper and become angry when, after waiting patiently, you finally get the salesperson's attention, only to have him or her dismiss you with a curt remark and make not even the slightest effort to be helpful?

A woman we know, Jane W., told us about finding herself in that particular situation one hectic Christmas season. After the saleswoman had dealt brusquely with several other customers, who left in a huff, it was Jane's turn. Jane asked to see some scarves in a variety of sizes and colors, as she wished to purchase several for gifts.

Carelessly flipping three scarves onto the counter, the saleswoman said, ''These are all we've got.'' But her tone of voice communicated that she really didn't want to spend much time with Jane.

''I was annoyed, but instead of getting rude right back, I tried to think of something sympathetic to say to her,'' Jane told us. ''I said, 'It must take a lot of patience to do this job.' Do you know what happened? She turned to me and said in a warmer voice, 'Boy, it really does. You won't believe the kind of people I have to put up with.' Then she told me about a few incidents she'd had with unpleasant customers that day. Before I knew it, I was really feeling empathy for her. I said, 'It's admirable the way you work at being patient. It must take a lot of control and a lot of effort.' She said, 'It really does.' Her voice softened, and she began bringing out more scarves than I'd ever expected to be able to choose from. It was a good feeling.''

Jane had changed the harried saleswoman into a nice, civil, agreeable person instead of letting herself be turned into another mean, arrogant, nasty customer. Like most of us, Jane likes to think of herself as a

thoughtful, considerate, likable human being who is
truly concerned about other people. When she is not
that way—when she is behaving in a way that contra-
dicts that good self-image—she feels bad about herself.
And it is usually because she has allowed someone else
to have control over her.

The whole key to not letting somebody else have control over you, making you do something that you would
not ordinarily do, is to *avoid reacting to what that person has said.* Of course, if it's something you would
normally do, that's fine. But doing something you
would not normally do is not fine at all, because then
you have allowed yourself to be changed from the way
you generally visualize yourself.

Like Jane, you really have the power to change other
people, but only if you don't let them get to you with
emotion-packed words.

The other side of the same coin is that if you are trying to motivate others, don't use emotion-packed words
on them.

"I'll give you my views, but I don't like being stereo-
typed as a woman. I'm here as one of the team," Laura
G. protested when one of the men she worked with
asked her for "the woman's point of view." Of course,
Laura had allowed herself to be distracted by the emotion-packed words and lost sight of the main point: that
they were all trying to make a decision. It would have
been more constructive for her to say to herself, "This is
emotion-packed. But it really doesn't matter whether or
not he was insulting me. We are trying to make a decision." Then she would have been able to communicate
more effectively and could have taken advantage of an
opportunity to advance up the company ladder rather
than gaining a reputation, from her bad reaction, for
being testy and oversensitive. The men in the company
became reluctant to talk to her at meetings for fear of
saying something she might misconstrue. As a result,
she had trouble moving ahead with her career objectives
and rationalized her problems by saying she worked for

a group of chauvinistic men. She didn't understand that by reacting to emotion-packed words, she had given the control to the group. She hadn't yet come to realize that other women were managing to get ahead by learning to deal with it and by playing the game. She brought misfortune on herself.

However, the fact remains that many business encounters must be made with people whom we consider too sensitive, too defensive or too apt to take things personally, so you'd best be aware or be prepared to accept the consequences. The readily identifiable overly sensitive person who is very verbal about his objection to unintended slurs has a counterpart in the person who won't react at the time but will later. It happens often in business.

A lion and a monkey having a business meeting with a rhinoceros and an elephant wouldn't need to be reminded to cool it with the nose jokes. It would be obvious. But in the business jungle, sensitivities may not be as evident or as subject to instant retaliation.

George W. lost an important sale while making small talk with a prospective client. "Some Jewish customers took me to a French restaurant last night, and you know, they really knew what to order," he said to Mr. Green over their business lunch.

Mr. Green thought to himself, Why did he say "Some Jewish customers took me to dinner last night?" Would he have said "Some Presbyterian customers took me to dinner" or "Some Baptist customers took me to dinner"? If he had said, "Some Jewish customers took me to dinner at a Jewish restaurant," that would have made sense.

Mr. Green felt that George had singled out Jews as a group and decided that George was anti-Semitic. He might have been altogether wrong about George, but he didn't want to do any business with him after that. Maybe Mr. Green was overly sensitive, but the salesman lost the account with him just the same. And he never knew why.

Whether you are the manager or the managed, the

salesperson or the customer, the more certain route to success with other people is to bring out the best in them. Condition yourself, heighten your awareness of the sensitivities of others and practice constantly until it becomes a completely natural thing for you to do. The more you use your awareness, the more you let it work *for* you, the more you will find yourself *wanting* to heighten it until doing so becomes as automatic a function for you as breathing in and out.

Attune yourself to everyday situations that open the door to the *unconscious use of emotion-packed words.* When you walk into an office and see a woman, don't automatically assume she is a secretary and ask her, "Who's in charge here?" If she answers, "I am," you're already in trouble.

A big problem for many people is the tendency to assume that everyone else is just like them. For instance, if off-color jokes don't bother you, you might assume that everyone else feels the same way and start sharing a few of your favorites, intending only to be amusing. But while these jokes are enjoyed by some people, they are a real turn-off for others. You should be able to find out these things about people, but an excellent rule of thumb is, If in doubt, don't!

Perhaps at your work place or in your private life, you are accustomed to using a lot of slang words or profanity in your ordinary speech. It's an acceptable way of communicating in that group. However, you should never assume that other people like such words too. Younger people in particular may be accustomed to using certain words within their peer group. But they are mistaken if they continue to use them in the business world, where they are communicating with people of different generations who could find such words offensive.

Another area of sensitivity is the use of names. In some situations people like to be called by their first names; in others they very definitely do not. If you walk into a business setting and call everyone by last name when it is the norm in that company to use first names, you may only be intending to show respect, but to the others you could be seen as lacking confidence. On the other hand, if you call others by their first names when everybody else is using last names, you could be misread as being brash and having a lack of sensitivity.

Perhaps you, like many of us, were told to commit to memory the adage Never talk religion or politics with anyone! We don't agree. We think religion and politics can make for some wonderful discussions. The only problem is with whom you are having the discussion. Discretion is the key. If you know that someone gets terribly emotional whenever the subject of politics comes up, don't discuss politics with that person. In the same context, don't discuss religion with somebody who only wants to convert you, will not have an open mind and cannot really *discuss* religion with you.

There are many kinds of emotion-packed words which, the instant you hear them, should automatically raise a mental warning flag that means, "Don't react!" When someone uses the royal "we," as in "*We* have a job to do," you know what is really meant is that *you* have the job to do. Or, as in that infamous hospital pronouncement, "*We* are going to take *our* temperature," you understand very well who is really going to get what done to whom.

When you hear someone say, "*They* said we're going to do it this way," you should ask yourself and the person who made the statement, "Who are *they?*"

Be on the alert for people who follow up everything you say in a meeting with, "What Bill is trying to say is . . ." and ask yourself if you really need anyone to amplify on what you're trying to say.

Don't let people make you angry by talking down to you, distorting your position or telling you how you feel about something. For example, "I *know* you feel badly about not getting that new opening in Saskatchewan." Maybe you don't feel that way at all. Maybe you didn't want to relocate right now or didn't feel ready for the added responsibility at this point in your career. Maybe for your own reasons, you're really feeling great about it!

Don't let your time and talents be wasted by people who ask for your advice when you know they're not going to take it, or by people who ask questions and never wait for the answers.

Be on your guard against your own bad reaction to attacking words like *stupid, dumb* and *gross*, and don't attack back. The word *you* followed by a negative verb, as in "You didn't tell me" . . . "You didn't hear me" . . . "You didn't listen," has an accusatory tone.

Watch out for dogmatic declarations like "It can't be done," as well as "We've always done it this way."

Listen for generalizing words like *all*, as in "All men do this," or "All women are alike," and for the word *everyone*, as in "Everyone knows that."

It isn't possible for us to include here every word, phrase or thought that everyone finds emotion-packed. But even if it were possible to do so, it is unlikely that our list would be completely applicable for everyone, as we have found that there are no absolutes. There isn't anything that is totally right or totally wrong. All people are different and what may be emotion-packed for one is not for another.

We do believe, however, that by beginning with this information and adding your own controls and your judgment of the situation, you will be able to start building your own list, increasing your success with other people as your own awareness and sensitivity grow.

Emotion-Packed Phrases to Avoid

Study the following list. Review it periodically. Add your own emotion-packed words to it as you learn what they are.

After all I've done for you.

Okay, okay, okay.

What difference does that make?

Let me be perfectly honest.

I wish you would say what you mean.

After you've been here as long as I have . . .

When I was your age . . .

If I were you . . .

Do you know what you're doing?

You aren't upset, are you?

Boss.

Superior.

Subordinate.

Shut up.

Company man.

Any very opinionated statement.

Any pretentious language.

Do you know what I mean?

I assumed that you knew.

Talk to me later.

Not to change the subject . . .

Do you understand me?

I wouldn't do that.

You wouldn't understand.

Are you sure that's right?

You don't mind, do you?

Girl.

Honey.

Broad.

Well . . .

So?

Any racial slur.

Taking God's name in vain.

· 7 ·

Find and Capitalize on
Points of Agreement
(Point, Counter-Point)

At 5 A.M. the tenant in apartment D turned his radio on full blast and Margo N., in apartment C, was once again rudely and prematurely awakened from a sound sleep. This had been happening every morning for the last two weeks, ever since the new neighbor had moved in across the hall, and Margo had had about all she could take. She was enraged. Quickly pulling on a shirt and jeans, she crossed the hall and pounded on the door of apartment D. A disheveled-looking young man opened it.

"Yes?" he asked sleepily.

"I've asked you as politely as I can not to turn that radio on so loud, and you just ignore me," Margo shouted. "Now I'm serious! This has got to stop!"

"And I've told you as politely as I can," the man retorted, "that I am a deep sleeper and I have to turn the clock-radio up loud or I won't hear it. I turn it off as soon as I wake up and that's the best I can do."

"I will not stand for this another minute," Margo screamed. "I've tried to be nice, but now I'm going to get you evicted, do you hear me?"

Without giving him a chance to reply, Margo stormed

back to her own apartment and slammed the door. Then she began to cry.

The truth is that Margo likes to think of herself as a reasonable, agreeable person, but right now she feels ashamed and even a little scared because she lost *control* and became an attacking, shouting person. She also knows that now she will have to do what she threatened to do: complain to the apartment management about the new tenant's loud radio. A clause in the lease prohibits noises of any kind that disturb other tenants, so the man in apartment D will either have to find some other way of waking up or he will have to move out. Margo can't help hoping he will leave, because if he stays, there will probably be other problems. The gauntlet is down, and she and the neighbor are committed to being adversaries. Since neither of them was really listening to the other, they were unable to look for a point of agreement.

Margo's reaction is not at all uncommon. While complaining may seem to come naturally to some people, Margo, like many of us, was taught early in life that it isn't nice to complain, it is impolite to insist and downright ugly to demand. In any conflict she starts out with that handicap and nets the same unsatisfactory results. She always ends up behaving in a manner counter to the way she likes to see herself.

Later that day, while having lunch with her closest friend, Margo will tell her friend about the incident and how bad she feels that the whole thing happened. Then she will ask her friend, "What else could I do?" This frustration is a common feeling.

The incident might have been avoided if Margo had kept control and looked for a point of agreement. The neighbor is a deep sleeper, and that is a serious problem. She is a light sleeper, and that too is a serious problem. They could easily agree that they both have problems. Now that they were empathizing with each other, it wouldn't be too difficult to brainstorm and find some solution that was acceptable to both. This might even have been the beginning of a new friendship.

People in business sometimes have to call other business people to make a complaint on behalf of their company. Often they have to listen to and resolve complaints from their company's customers. Arnold E., a new employee in the billing department of Tri-Cities Utility Company, became involved in such a problem when he received a phone call from an irate consumer.

"This is Edward B., and I live at 2008 Bellringer Drive. I'm calling about my fuel bill for last month," the angry voice on the telephone said. "There's absolutely no way you can convince me that I used all that fuel. Why, I wasn't even at home half the time. How can it cost that much to heat an unoccupied house? You've obviously made a mistake."

"Actually, Mr. B., your bill was no higher than most of your neighbors' bills were," Arnold replied defensively. "Besides, you must have used that much or we wouldn't have charged you for it. After all, this company doesn't want to cheat anyone."

"Well, I think I'm being robbed, and I'm not going to stand for it!" Mr. B. shouted.

"That's up to you, Mr. B., but if you don't pay your bill, we will have to cut off your service," Arnold said. At that Mr. B. slammed the telephone down loudly. Then he called Arnold's supervisor to complain that he had "an extremely poor attitude towards the customers" and had "threatened to discontinue service" to Mr. B.'s home.

Speaking in a conciliatory tone of voice, the supervisor asked Mr. B. about the problem that had prompted his first call. She listened until he was finished, then she said, "Mr. B., I can understand your concern about the meter reading, especially since you say you weren't heating your home half the time. I can send someone out in the morning to verify the reading and make sure the meter is working as it should." Then she assured him that she would personally contact him by tomorrow afternoon to report the results and work out some resolution of the dispute. Mr. B. was placated but, like Margo, he wasn't feeling good about himself either.

What went wrong? First of all, Mr. B., in following his visceral feeling that the Tri-Cities Utility Company was his enemy, unwisely chose to take the offensive. All he accomplished by doing that was to put Arnold on the defensive, and that was certain death for their communication. Mr. B. failed to keep *control*. He could have used other phrases that stated exactly what he wanted while being supportive of Arnold. He could have said, "I know you are very careful about billing; perhaps the problem is the meter," instead of attacking with words like "There's no way you can convince me." Had he kept control, he probably would have gotten what he wanted without getting nasty.

Arnold had heard only Mr. B.'s complaint and the anger in his voice and had reacted badly by becoming defensive and insisting that the billing was correct. If Arnold had been *listening for a point of agreement,* as his supervisor had done, he would have also heard Mr. B. say that he thought there must have been a mistaken reading of his meter. He then could have offered to send someone out to read it again, and Mr. B. would not have made the second call to complain about Arnold.

The supervisor kept control because she *listened for the point of agreement*. She followed the three basic rules essential for finding points of agreement: the points must be honest, they must be verbalized, and there must be no *buts*.

The person who uses points of agreement will never say, "But he *knew* how I felt," or "She *should have known* that I agreed." There are no such assumptions; everything has to be *said*. People like to be patted on the back once in a while, and they want to be recognized. One of the best ways to do that is simply to *tell* them. The more you speak the language of success, the more you will learn to be aware of the ways you create a positive climate and of the ways other people will react to it.

Most people walk into business meetings listening for points of *disagreement*. They've been conditioned that way—to approach each other with a what's-going-on-here, let's-see-what's-wrong attitude. So of course they find what they're looking for and they disagree. Then they say that they disagree, and they get the negativism going back and forth.

But you can change everything if you take to the meeting an attitude of *listening for points of agreement*. That means *really listening*. Many times in meetings we don't listen to anybody else. We hear one word that we don't agree with and we start dwelling on it because we just can't wait to get up and argue about the word. In the rest of the statement, the person may have said almost everything we wanted to say, but we didn't hear him because he said one or two things we didn't like. At that point we stopped listening.

Frequently two opposing ideas will be presented at the conference table, with very poor results. To illustrate, consider what happened when Harry presented his idea: "We've got a terrific product here, and we should spend $10,000 to advertise it in a national magazine."

Jack doesn't completely agree with Harry's proposal. Without *control* he might say, "I think that's a terrible idea, and I think we'd do better by spending that money on door-to-door samples."

Jack has used emotion-packed words. He has made Harry angry, and he has pushed them both into corners where Harry has to defend national magazines and Jack has to defend door-to-door samples. The peer group has stopped thinking about what's good for the product, and they're taking sides with one or the other of these two men, whose egos are now on the line. Whatever happens after that, the meeting has been ruined. The two men are reacting negatively to each other.

But what if Jack had had *control* and had *listened for points of agreement*? He might have said, "Yes, I agree that we have an excellent product here and that we should spend $10,000 to advertise it. I'd like to examine your proposition thoroughly, and I would like us to consider some other options as well, such as door-to-door samples."

Now he has found two *honest* points of agreement. He has *verbalized* them clearly so that everyone has heard them, and he has introduced his own idea with *no "but"* preceding it.

Jack has made Harry feel important by listening to him and then agreeing that he had a good idea. Now Harry, in turn, can really listen to Jack's proposal without getting his ego involved. When Jack is really supportive of Harry and listens to him, letting him know that he really respects his thinking, then Harry, even without realizing it, wants to do the same for Jack. The difference of opinion has been elevated to a professional, businesslike level. Now everyone at the table can be receptive and can participate freely, without polarizing.

Anita R. told us how she had successfully applied this listening technique recently during an exchange with her son. Michael had telephoned from college and said, "Mother, I'm coming home this weekend but I think I'll leave my car here at school."

"I said, 'That's great, Michael. We're looking forward to seeing you. But why don't you leave your car with your sister? I know she could really use it to take her laundry to be done and run some other errands.'

"Michael started yelling at me. 'What? Are you kidding? Leave my car with her? My brand-new car that doesn't have a mark on it? No way! I'd rather drive it home than leave it with her.'

"Years ago I think I would probably have gotten angry at him and said something like, 'Michael, why are you so selfish? Why aren't you willing to do anything for anyone else? We're always doing things for you, but you never care about us. I insist that you leave your car for your sister to use.'

"And he would have done one of two things. Since we're paying for his schooling, he would have obediently and reluctantly left his car, come home and made all our lives miserable all weekend. Or, being twenty-one years old and kind of independent, he would have brought the car home with him anyway, and I would have had to make his life miserable all weekend.

"Instead, when he started yelling at me like that, I thought to myself, This is emotion-packed, and I didn't start yelling back at him. I got control because I didn't yell. The second thing I did was to *listen for the point of agreement*, and that was that he really had taken good care of that car.

"I was now able to say, 'Michael, you're right. Dad and I are so proud of you, the way you've taken care of that car. We are really impressed.' Michael calmed down and stopped yelling.

"I said to him, 'Michael, I think you've got a problem. You're a great brother, and we both agree you are very fond of your sister. I remember how I felt about getting the first dent in my new car. You have to weigh which is more important: risking a dent by being generous or playing it safe. I can't make the decision for you.' "

By *listening for the point of agreement* and *verbalizing* it to Michael, Anita had raised the discussion to a rational level. Neither she nor Michael felt backed into a corner, and Michael became more receptive to Anita because she had made him *feel good*. Anita, in turn, was in a more receptive state also, where she was less likely to say something she didn't care to have to live with. Even if Michael had chosen not to do what Anita hoped he would, at the very least they would both have had a more pleasant weekend visit. In fact, he did leave the car for his sister.

When *control* is lost, tempers can flare on both sides and people will often say and do things they would never say or do under ordinary circumstances. Then, even though the particular conflict or problem may eventually be resolved, everyone is deprived of the good feelings that could have resulted from having resolved it well.

If you can keep *control* and *really listen* to what someone has to say, and find out what you can agree with, and use that as the basis of what you want to say, it can be very helpful. Again, we are not saying that you should be insincere, and we are not saying never to disagree with anyone. But you shouldn't have to be anything but open and honest if you are willing to listen hard enough.

Keep in mind the three basic rules of listening for points of agreement:

1. Always be sincere. Don't try to fabricate a phony point of agreement.
2. Verbalize the point of agreement when you find it.
3. No *buts*. Don't say you agree *but*, and then proceed to disagree.

· 8 ·
Listen for the Hidden Agenda (Listening Between the Lines)

A man who had been listening to his police radio reported hearing the following dispatch: "Any car in area, go to parking lot, Cedar Bend Apartments, check report of sixty-six-year-old man sitting on curb unclothed." The listener wondered, among other things, how the man's age was known. Approximately five minutes later this follow-up call came over the radio: "Car checking parking lot of Cedar Bend, correction of first report. Check '66 Chevrolet parked by curb. Has been stripped."

It's easy to spot our "thirty percent listener" here. He took action—began his report—without listening for all the information. But what about all the information we encounter in life, when the full story is not always evident in the words alone?

The average toothpaste commercial on television is definitely sending us two messages. The *words* tell us "Buy our product; it's good for your teeth." The hidden message is "If you use our product, you will be beautiful and successful."

In many forms of communication, running the gamut

from novels to newspaper and television advertising, we have become attuned to the possibility of double meaning: the first expressed in the actual words we see or hear; the second between the lines.

But advertisers are not alone in their exploitation of the power of the hidden message. For example, economists talk about a *normalizing business cycle* instead of a *boom* or a *bust*, and the stock market sometimes goes into a *technical correction* instead of a *plunge*. There are many levels, both conscious and unconscious, on which we all deal daily with hidden messages.

You meet one of your neighbors in the parking lot at the shopping center.

"Hello, how are you?"

"Just fine, thanks. And you?"

"Okay."

"That's good. Well, see you around."

"Take care, now."

You know that people really do converse like that without giving a thought to the meaning or meaning a word of what they say. So many everyday situations suggest certain standard remarks that we use automatically, without thinking, and that are accepted in the same spirit by the other person.

For example, you meet someone from another office in the elevator on your way to work.

"Hi, what's new?"

"Nothing much. You?"

"Same old thing."

Every evening on the sidewalk in front of the office building, as you leave for the day, you meet some of the same people.

"See you tomorrow."

"Have a good evening."

These are social rituals, act/react communications, with *hidden messages* to which no one really expects any other response but the usual ones. The hidden messages behind these brief communications are simple: "I am giving you a friendly greeting," and "I acknowledge your friendly greeting and return it." It's the same as in all the many other standard salutations, such as "How's tricks?" "What's happening?" "How's it going?" and "How's business?" And in the usual parting words like "See you soon," "Have a good day," "Nice talking to you," and even "Don't take any wooden nickels."

These verbal social rituals have become so ingrained that we'd never expect anyone to break the pattern by really answering, by saying something like, "Well, that depends. Physically I suppose I'm okay, but emotionally I'm all torn up. Which would you rather hear about?" We would be startled at first, then amused if he was only joking. But if he actually launched into a dissertation on the state of his well-being, we'd be annoyed and maybe even bored if he went on in too much detail. We might even be late for work. Most of us, however, follow the rules in casual encounters like these, both giving and receiving the benevolent hidden message in the fewest possible words.

If the greeting is meant to be a prelude to a real conversation, then there are other hidden messages that will imply this and other rules that will apply. We won't go into them here. We wish only to point out here that these ritual hidden messages do no harm and often even serve positive social purposes, such as breaking the ice between strangers or being a form of friendly affirmation or an offering of caring. We would also like to point out that whether you have been aware of it or not, you have constantly been giving and receiving hidden messages.

Parents and children exchange hidden messages all the time. For example, when Timmy's mother notices that Timmy has been quiet for quite a while, she calls out, "Timmy, what are you doing?" He hears the anxiety in her voice and he guesses he could be in trouble for painting on his bedroom walls.

"Nothing," he answers. He knows it isn't true, and Mother knows that she'd better go and see what he is up to. Timmy can't understand how Mother "always knows." He doesn't understand that what Mother has learned to do is ignore the words and tune in to the hidden message behind them. Combining what she hears with her "third ear" and what she has learned about Timmy's behavior patterns, Mother comes up with the right answer. This process requires that you be a very good listener and know something about the message sender.

Loving couples often exchange hidden messages. Consider:

"You're very quiet. What are you thinking about?" he asks her as they sit gazing up at the starry sky. (Translation: "Are you thinking about the same thing I'm thinking about?")

"Oh, nothing," she replies shyly. (Translation: "I want to see if you care enough to coax me.")

"Ah, come on, tell me," he coaxes, catching the hidden message. "Tell me what you're thinking." (Translation: "Got your message and have responded. Now it's your turn.")

"Well," she says, her cheeks a little flushed, "I was just thinking . . ." (Translation: "I got your message. Now . . .")

The hidden messages may change a little after the bloom wears off the romance, but they still work the same way.

"Is something bothering you?" he asks, noticing that she is unusually quiet. (Translation: "I have the feeling you're mad at me, but I'm not sure I really want to know.")

"Nothing you'd be interested in," she says, turning to stare out the window at the rain as she waits for him to insist. (Translation: "Yes, I am angry at you and I'm glad you noticed, but don't think I'm going to make it any easier on you just because you asked. Besides, I want you to figure it out yourself.")

"Well, if you don't want to talk about it, there's nothing I can do about it," he says. (Translation: "Now I know I've done something wrong, and I'm really afraid to ask.")

Close friends send and receive hidden messages. Helen had a lot of things on her mind that afternoon when her friend Loretta picked her up.

"Oh, Loretta, I've got so much to do that I don't see how I can get it all done on time. I've got to get everything packed and ready for the move to the new house next week and get the kids transferred to the new school, and the volunteers bureau called to remind me it's my turn to run the thrift shop tomorrow," Helen said. "And you know how they resent it when we put them in a bind by not sticking to the schedule. But I just forgot to let them know in time that I wouldn't be available. It's all my own fault, but I don't know what I'm going to do."

Loretta turned to Helen and said, "Are you trying to ask me to take your place at the thrift shop tomorrow?"

Helen thought for a moment, then said, "Yes, now that you mention it, I probably was asking, although I didn't realize it at the time. I thought I was just unloading my concern about how I was going to meet that obligation. You're a very good friend to have picked up on that."

"Okay, I'll do it," Loretta said.

"No, it wouldn't be fair to ask you," Helen said. "You've got plenty to do also."

"I can manage it," Loretta said. "I'll do it."

Helen really needed Loretta's help, but she didn't want to *ask* and put Loretta in the position of either having to say no or of feeling obligated by friendship to say yes. So on an unconscious level, Helen poured out her problems, with a *hidden message* that said "I hope you will help me."

All of us often use this method unconsciously, the way Helen did, so that we can avoid putting ourselves in the position of having to ask and putting the other person in the position of having to turn us down.

Professional negotiators rely very heavily on hidden messages, even though they follow a strict procedure that is known to both sides. Actually the procedure itself is rife with crucial hidden messages. If someone breaks the rules, the result can be chaotic to the procedure, costly to the side that broke the rules and disastrous to the career of the rule breaker.

The standard scenario requires that each negotiator come to the table knowing what he wants, what he will offer, what he will reject and how much of a concession he will make. Each side knows that the other has that information but will not give it in a straightforward manner and that he will really have to listen for the hidden messages in what the other side says in order to receive the clues. Ideally the mutual goal is an agreement that will meet the needs of both sides as nearly as possible.

Negotiations take place on every level of our lives, both personal and business: in living rooms, meeting rooms, bedrooms, courtrooms, in new- and used-car showrooms and real-estate offices, just to name a few places. They take place between neighbors and between governments. Many negotiators have interested parties who are indirectly involved, such as children, parents, co-workers, higher-ups or boards of directors. The hidden messages can become very complex.

In a business setting people say things that can have a number of possible meanings and for which there may be no rules to guide you. The other person may give you the hidden message either with or without being aware of doing it. In these situations you will have to rely on your listening skills to become aware that there is a hidden message, and then you will have to go fishing for it.

Someone comes into your office and says, "I'm exhausted. Last night and the night before and the night before that, I was here until ten o'clock, and I'm really tired." You, as that person's manager, must decide to take that statement and search for the hidden message, if only because there is a good chance there may be other messages you should know about.

That person could be sending this hidden message: "I really need some help. I know I was hired to do this job myself, and I'm afraid that if I tell you that I need a helper, you're going to think that I'm not doing a good job for you. So I won't tell you right out. I won't say it that way, but instead I'll just tell you how much extra work I've been handling.''

Another hidden message might be: ''On my last job evaluation, you talked to me about my attitude, and you said that you expected everyone to put in some extra work, to make an extra effort, and I just want to be sure that you *know* that I am doing what you asked.''

Another hidden message could be: ''I am a little worried about my job security, so I want you to see what a dedicated employee I am.''

Still another might be: ''I want a pat on the back. I want you, as my supervisor, to say, 'I know that you've done this, and I recognize and appreciate your effort.' ''

You should be able to find out which hidden message is behind that ''I'm exhausted.'' Len B. knew how to do that. Len, a successful insurance executive, noticed that his secretary seemed unusually constrained. Sensing that she might be unhappy about something work related, Len asked Amy to come into his office for a talk.

''Amy, you and I have always worked very well together and with mutual respect during our four years of association,'' Len began. ''However, I have the feeling lately that you are not as happy with our relationship as you have been in the past. Something seems to be troubling you enough that it is affecting your job performance, too, and I'm very concerned. Am I in any way responsible for this change in our relationship?''

''No, of course not,'' Amy answered quickly. ''It's nothing *you've* done.''

Len heard the emphasis Amy put on *you*, took that as a possible clue and decided to pursue it further.

''Do you feel that you have too much of a workload?'' Len asked, trying to find out if Amy needed help but didn't want to ask for it.

''No, my workload is reasonable, just as it is for *everyone* who is willing to put in a day's work,'' Amy said in a flat voice. Another clue.

''Do you feel that you are being paid a fair salary?''

Len asked, still searching for the problem.

"Yes," Amy said coolly, then added, "All of us are being paid more than fairly for our jobs *here*." More clues.

Len knew enough now to make an educated guess at what was bothering Amy. He had heard the emphasis Amy put on certain words, the way in which Amy kept including the other office workers in what she said and her obvious reluctance to state the problem outright.

"Amy, do you have an outside job?" Len asked.

"Absolutely not. *I* know the company's policy against *that*," Amy said emphatically.

Now Len could guess the rest. He did a little discreet investigating and found out that several of the newer employees were violating company policy by working part-time at other jobs. Len then checked their attendance records through their personnel folders, and it became apparent that they were also using their paid sick days to do this. It was an open secret in the office, and everyone's morale was being affected adversely. But Amy, as a long-time and loyal employee, not only resented what was going on, but she wanted her boss to know about it. She wanted him to take action, so that she could continue to have his respect for her professionalism.

Once Len had searched out the hidden messages Amy was giving him, he took appropriate action to stop the moonlighting of the other employees. As soon as he did that, his good working relationship with Amy was restored and Amy's job performance improved.

If hidden messages aren't listened for, they can easily escape detection and attention, and the next hidden message may be delivered in the form of a resignation. The reason given to the boss or the personnel office generally will not be what the employee really has in mind. The stated reason may be dissatisfaction with salary, and that might be true to some extent, but it probably isn't the real reason for quitting. The true but hidden message is more likely to be something like the feeling of not having a future with the company or of not being able to move ahead. That employee has probably not been getting enough positive feedback but is uncomfortable about saying that, so he chooses something he can talk about, even if it isn't what he really would like to say.

Many times when employees talk about money, the real problem is that the working situation is awful or they hate the boss. Surveys indicate that people who leave their jobs with a complaint about salary often take jobs that actually pay even less but that seem to offer them more opportunity to move ahead or a work environment in which they are happier.

Hidden messages are not exclusively passed upward to management. They are also passed downward, from management. Some employees become very skilled at listening for and interpreting the hidden messages that are sent out by the people above them in the organization.

Lester R., a manager of a large manufacturing company, told us that he often goes to meetings at which his boss doesn't tell him exactly what he wants done. But Lester has learned to listen for the hidden messages in what his employer does say, which tell him that the boss wants a certain person fired or a policy unofficially augmented.

This is essentially the same sort of thing we see done with frequency in politics and government, when, for example, the President's staff members *perceive* what they *think* the President wants done and act accordingly.

Sometimes they're right and sometimes they're wrong. Sometimes the man in charge does this purposely so that if it works out well, he can accept the credit. But if it goes wrong, he can deny any knowledge of it and he has a scapegoat. The employee who misinterprets the hidden message is categorized as "making bad decisions" or "showing poor judgment." But the employee who does this well is invaluable and can move quickly up the corporate or political ladder.

Now we are not suggesting that one should go around

analyzing everything everybody says. What we are suggesting is that this is one more aspect of good listening that can be understood and used to your advantage and the advantage of others you deal with every day.

Occasionally you will be wrong and see a hidden message where none was intended. But if you are in *control* and can pull this technique out at the appropriate times and *listen for the hidden message*, you will get excellent results.

Listening between the lines—to what's being said *behind* the words—is one of the most helpful tools of the verbal inventory. A result of learning this skill can be an unexpected windfall of information or opportunity for the accomplished listener.

· 9 ·

Don't Get Taken In by
False Signals
(When Yes Means No)

A first cousin to the hidden message is the *false signal,*
which usually involves some deception. Take an ordinary game of poker:

"All right, fellas," Ed said as he shuffled the cards.
"The game is five-card draw and nothing's wild." He
passed the deck to Don for a cut, then dealt all around.
The mood at the table turned serious.

"I'll bet one dollar," Al said.

Bob said, "I'll see your dollar and raise you two."

"I call," Cliff said, tossing in two chips. Don, without commenting, did the same thing.

"I'll see you and raise you two more," Ed said
casually.

Then Al, Bob and Cliff each took three new cards,
discarding three from their hands. Don looked at his
hand, then took one new card and discarded one. Then
Ed took two cards and discarded two, and found himself holding three kings and two queens: a full house. Ed
swallowed hard and kept his face expressionless while he
did some heavy thinking. He figured from their moves
that Al, Bob and Cliff were each holding a pair and that

Don was trying for a straight or a flush. That would mean that Ed was in a very fortunate position.

Al made another one-dollar bet, and Bob raised him two dollars. Cliff folded. Don raised again, to three dollars. The stakes were almost at the limit they had all agreed on.

Ed *knew* that he was holding the winning hand. As dealer, he was in the ideal position, because everyone else would have to make his bet and lay his cards on the table before him. So he raised again, going to the full limit of the game.

And then they all put their cards on the table. Al showed a pair of aces. Bob had a pair of jacks and a pair of sixes. So far, so good, for Ed and he was feeling like a winner. Then Don showed four deuces and Ed, poor Ed, knew that he had been had. As the last few minutes flashed before his mind's eye, he realized that when Don had called and taken only one card he was bluffing. When Don had looked at his cards, put them face-down on the table instead of holding them and sat very quietly, unsmiling, he was using his body language to reinforce the message he wanted to send: the false signal that he was holding a weak hand. He had been holding the four deuces all that time, and Ed had just never considered the possibility.

In many ways the game of poker is analogous to the game we call life. And the false signals, like the ones Don sent, aren't basically unlike the false signals in other life situations. Some of the phrases from poker are even borrowed and used descriptively in life situations: poker face, straight man, setup, open and shut, holding the winning hand and playing your cards close to your chest. We have borrowed phrases from many sources to add color to our verbal communications, and many of them, not too surprisingly, apply to the false signal.

The truth is that we are all very vulnerable to the many kinds of false signals we are given all the time, and we even respond to some of them on an unconscious level. We often *see* and defer to false signals. Many a visitor has been able to gain access to a patient's room after hospital visiting hours by wearing a stethoscope casually draped around his neck or tucked carelessly into his pocket. We are often impressed by the authority of uniforms, from the starched white lab coat to the brass-buttoned military jacket. We even employ a little harmless deception ourselves when we dress prosperously for an appointment to obtain a bank loan or go back to work with a sun-lamp tan after a stay-home vacation.

We know that a black bag or stethoscope do not a doctor make and that a military-looking uniform with all the fittings can be rented or purchased, but we don't usually think about it. We usually accept them for what they seem to be.

Sometimes we suspend our disbelief for a period of time; for example, while we are watching a performance. We allow the actors and actresses to convince us of almost anything. We know very well that what we are seeing and hearing is not real, but we have willingly gone to see the film or play, and as long as the performers do reasonably well at entertaining us, we enjoy the illusion for as long as it lasts. However, as soon as we leave the theater or turn off the television, we bring ourselves back to reality and some healthy skepticism. And that little bit of healthy skepticism is very important. In real life, just as in a theatrical performance, things are not always as they seem to be, and it would be a mistake to assume that they are.

Malcolm Baldridge, former chairman and chief executive officer of Scoville Inc., of Waterbury, Connecticut, once told a public relations group that he doubted that many of the people who use multisyllabic words and phrases really understand what they are saying.

"There is a kind of protection in a statement or a recommendation so vague that it can be interpreted two or three ways on a single issue," Baldridge said, and added, "That's not communicating; it's covering one's flanks."

So it should not have been a surprise that when Baldridge went to Washington, D.C., to serve as secretary of commerce in the Reagan administration, he grasped the opportunity to put his beliefs into action. One of the things he did was have some of the word-processing equipment in his department programmed to respond to certain vague words and phrases. On his list of forbiddens are: *ongoing, orient, effectuated, input, institutionalized, interface, maximize, parameter, responsive, thrust, specificity, utilize, hopefully, prioritize, therein, enclosed within, untimely death, I would hope, as I am sure you know, as you are aware, I share your concern, contingent upon, inappropriate, management regime* and *mutually beneficial*.

When one of these blackballed items appears in a Department of Commerce memo, the word processor stops and flashes a signal on the screen: "Don't use this word!"

Wouldn't it be helpful if each of us could have our own mental word processor to flash a warning whenever it heard a false signal coming or going? What we can do is *listen for the false signals*.

Learning to recognize false signals begins with an attitude of healthy skepticism, of not taking things for granted simply because they *appear* to be a certain way or because someone *sounds* like he or she is communicating a certain thing.

Dogs don't have the power to communicate verbally. They are popular as pets largely because they are the total, perfect listeners: nonjudgmental and nonadvising. We talk to them and they wag their tails, and we can put any meaning we choose into the tail-wagging. Dogs don't argue with us. But, among dogs, they know that there is a fine difference. When two dogs approach each other wagging their tails, they know that a wagging tail can be either a friendly greeting or a challenge to a fight, and each dog makes his own evaluation of the situation. It's possible that they occasionally misinterpret and find themselves on the losing end of an unwanted scrap, too. But no one is more surprised than the people who thought that since the dogs were wagging their tails, they were getting along fine. Like all false signals, the trouble with a wagging tail is that it only *implies*. It does not tell us anything directly. We can make a guess, but if we guess wrong we can find ourselves in an undesirable position, having made the wrong decision based on implied support or lack of it.

Many times at business meetings there are as many different ideas being presented and seeking support as there are people, and the signals can be confusing. When Constance R. presented her proposal to a group, a brief discussion followed, and then a vote was called for. Much to Constance's surprise, her proposal passed unopposed. But after the meeting, as everyone milled about in the hallway, commenting casually on the meeting, three of the people told Constance that they really didn't support her project, and so she should not depend on them for help.

"If you didn't agree with me, why didn't you speak up in the meeting?" Constance asked.

"Nobody asked," one of the three said, shrugging, and the others nodded in agreement. Because nobody had asked for their opinions and they hadn't been willing to volunteer anything, Constance had gotten what she wanted from the meeting without opposition. But she was also without some valuable support.

In business, managers sometimes give false signals to the people they supervise. Ruby L. thought she was a very lucky person to be working for her boss. He was very easy to get along with, and he made a point of complimenting everyone on something every day. He would laugh with them, and he was more like one of them than he was a supervisor. But when performance-evaluation time rolled around, Ruby and several of the other people she worked with were shocked to find out how dissatisfied their supervisor really was with their job performance. He had always been so kind and so understanding when they came in late or left early and when they made too many errors or didn't meet deadlines that they never expected to see those things show up as failings on their personnel records. He had been giving them false signals all along, implying that what they were doing was all right.

Sometimes companies will give off false signals that say, for example, "Go ahead and enjoy the expense account. When you're out of town you're working hard, and we expect you to spend forty or fifty dollars for dinner. We expect you to stay in a good room and to fly first class." The startling enlightenment comes when someone with more authority calls you into his office and says, "Don't you think you've been taking advantage of this company's generosity?" Because there were no rules and no company policy relevant to the limits of expense accounts, false signals were given.

A business dealing is not the time and a meeting room is not the place for suspending disbelief. Imagine now that you're in a meeting, in the midst of a very spirited discussion, and Bill over there is giving you all the signals implying that he thinks you are right and he is in agreement with you. He keeps nodding his head. He has made a few comments and has asked you a couple of pertinent questions that have given you opportunities to do some elaborating. He has said, "Tell me more about this," and "I'd like to hear a few more of your thoughts on that." He certainly sounds as though he wants you to sell your idea, so you go ahead and tell all. After a while you've told everything you know. You have put all your cards on the table about this idea of yours. You sit back to wait for the discussion. And then, to your dismay, Bill rips you apart!

Or another time it might be that as you present your idea, Joe is making comments like "I understand," or "I see what you mean." He certainly sounds like he's agreeing with you. When the time arrives to begin the discussion, you turn to Joe in anticipation of his support and say, "Joe, would you elaborate to the group? How do you feel about this?" And Joe knocks your socks off by coming out in opposition to you. Inwardly you groan because it was you who asked him to speak, and if you hadn't, he might not have expressed his disagreement. You got a false signal from things he said, which you now realize were just cover phrases. You mistakenly thought he was your ally and got stabbed in the back. It's bad enough that Joe spoke up at all, but it's even worse that it was you who encouraged him.

The false signals Bill and Joe sent might have been deliberate or they might not, but that really is beside the point. Either way, what has happened is that they have gotten you to commit yourself totally, saying everything you had to say, because you thought they were going along with you. And you finished only to find that *they* hadn't really committed a thing to your cause. Everything you *thought* they were willing to do, they were not. You are all alone on your sinking ship. Now you're damned if you do and damned if you don't, because if you go back and repeat something you've already said, you sound weak; but if you don't say anything at all, you sound weak. You need a whole new array of facts to save this one. You're sunk.

False signals are not exclusive to the business world. They also come into personal relationships. Consider, for example, all the false signals that men give to women and women give to men.

When Jack meets Jill and asks her to have dinner with him that night, all he has in mind is that he wants some company because he hates to eat alone. But because he wants Jill to agree to spend some time with him, he may coax her just a little more enthusiastically than his true feelings for her actually warrant. Jill, who is flattered by all his attentions and thinks he is absolutely charming, may think the invitation means that he likes her as much as she likes him. Jack means no harm, but Jill could be in for a big disappointment.

Georgeanne and Richard had known each other only a short time, but their relationship had intensified very quickly. Too quickly, Georgeanne thought, and so she suggested to Richard that they see less of each other and more of other people. Richard reluctantly agreed. Then Georgeanne called Richard on the telephone every night for long conversations. She stopped after Richard finally told her that she was confusing him by saying one thing and doing another.

Douglas had been dating Barbara for almost a year, and they both understood that he liked her "as a friend." But when his company told him they were sending him to San Francisco for a few days, he invited Barbara to come along with him and even offered to pay her expenses. Barbara told Douglas quite frankly that she would have to reconsider their relationship before she could accept that kind of offer, and she suggested that he also consider what he might be implying about her relative importance in his life. Douglas said that she was right, and that maybe she was more important to him than he had realized. On the other hand, if she wasn't that important, he should not act as though she was. He went to San Francisco alone to think it over.

Some people go looking for a kind of false signal that will support them in denying the truth. This happens frequently between doctors and patients.

When Gilbert V. was told by his doctor that he must stop smoking, he questioned the doctor's advice, hoping to find a weak link that would allow him to rationalize his continued smoking. If the doctor was not emphatic enough, Gilbert would decide, "Well, he really doesn't think it would be so bad if I don't quit right now." But Gilbert's doctor sends very clear signals and sticks to them. Gilbert attempted to force a compromise by gradually reducing his daily tobacco quota, with the expectation that the doctor at some point would agree that Gilbert had sacrificed enough. However, when Gilbert proudly proclaimed, "I am down to smoking only three cigarettes a day," his doctor answered, "If you're only smoking three cigarettes a day, you don't need any." Even Gilbert had no way of denying that clear a signal, and he stopped smoking.

Frequently parents and children will exchange false signals until something happens to upset the balance of their relationship. Darlene and Gregory W. had only one child—their son Corbett—and he was truly the apple of his mother's eye. Gregory had to travel a lot, with the result that Darlene had raised Corbett to manhood almost unassisted. When Corbett was in medical school, Darlene sent him extra money and whatever else he said he needed, because she wanted nothing to distract him from his studies. One day, when Gregory was away on an extended business trip and Darlene was feeling lonely, she telephoned Corbett to ask him if he could take her to dinner that evening. He said he was pleased that she had called, and he consented at once.

"Of course, Mother," he said amiably. "Alexis and I have a date for dinner tonight, but if you're coming along you can make reservations for us at a much nicer place."

"Wait a minute, Corbett," Darlene said. "I thought *you* were taking *me* to dinner."

"I am, Mother," he said. "I'm taking you out with Alexis and me. But you are going to pay for it, aren't you? You always do. Besides, I understood you to mean that you wanted me to take you out in the most literal sense."

Darlene was becoming angry. "If I wanted to treat you, Corbett, I would have said so. I rather expected that since you are now a practicing physician and now have an income of your own, you would be willing to treat *me*."

"Well, since you insist on making this an issue over money, why don't we settle it by going dutch?" Corbett suggested.

"I don't believe I want to go out for dinner after all," Darlene said and hung up the telephone. But she thought about the conversation all evening. And the more she thought about it, the more hurt she became. And the more she realized that she had always encouraged Corbett to think of himself first. She had made excuses and created false signals to avoid having to face the unpleasant reality. Darlene knew that she would have to change her own false signals to Corbett, which had always been telling him that it was all right for him to be a taker. She knew it would be a difficult and painful change for both of them.

If you have ever said yes when you meant no, you were giving a false signal. It happens between husbands and wives all the time. For example, they have been planning to go to the theater for a week and suddenly he asks, "Do you really feel like going out tonight?" And she says, "No, dear, not if you don't want to."

Or she says, as the new washer-and-dryer combination is being installed, "This will be my birthday present. You don't have to get me anything else for my birthday next month." On her birthday she's upset, and he's confused. "But you told me . . . !" he protests in vain.

Or he asks her if she would mind eating at the cafeteria instead of the favorite restaurant he promised, because it's more convenient and he doesn't feel like waiting for a table tonight. She hates cafeterias, but she says, "No, I don't mind." When he asks her later why she hardly touched her food, she says, "It's nothing. I just hate cafeterias. You know I hate cafeterias."

"Then why did you say yes?" he asks.

"Why did you ask?" she answers. "You know that if you ask I have to say yes!"

And therein lies a great, though simple, truth. It can even work in reverse, so that people feel they have to say no. When Jeannine slipped on her front steps one morning and broke her leg in two places, she was put in a cast and told to stay off her feet as much as possible for the next six weeks. Jeannine's friends called to express their sympathy and their desire to be helpful. But because they didn't want to seem to be forcing attention on her, they questioned her about her needs.

"Do you want me to come over?" they asked. "Is there anything I can do?"

"No, not really, I'm okay," Jeannine told them, just as most of us would have done. Anytime we're asked a question like that at a time like·that, the answer will probably be negative.

Certain questions asked in a business setting will automatically get the same false-signal response. For example:

"Would you mind finishing this for me so that I can leave early tonight?" Patrick asks for the third time in two weeks.

"No, I don't mind," Vera answers, feeling trapped and coerced by a question that was, intentionally or unintentionally, a loaded one. The "do you mind?" type of question is like a verbal version of the children's game of hide-and-seek. The question implies that there is a choice while actually obscuring it. Vera knows that the choice is there, but she can't get hold of it so she can't respond to it honestly. Vera feels compelled to say, again, "No, I don't mind," when actually she minds very much.

What can Jeannine and her friends, or Patrick and Vera, do if they want to stop playing communications hide-and-seek? They can begin to listen for those false signals and then, instead of just *reacting* to them, they can *deal* with them openly.

Jeannine could ask her friends, "What would you *like* to do for me?" Or her friends could volunteer, "We're going to come over and we're going to do your shopping for you. Make out your list."

Patrick could rephrase his request, making it reciprocal, such as, "If you will finish this for me so that I can leave early, I will return the favor anytime you choose." Or Vera could answer his "do you mind?" honestly. Not with an angry "you have a lot of nerve!" or "yes, dammit, I do mind!" But with a quiet, composed "Yes, Patrick, as a matter of fact, I do mind."

Jeannine would get the help that she really needed desperately, and her friends would feel pleased that they had truly been friends in need. Patrick would realize that he was imposing on Vera and would probably apologize, saying something like, "It was very thoughtless of me to ask you again. I hope you will let me return the favor sometime." All the false signals could be turned into more honest communications, probably strengthening the relationships.

Few of us are so naive these days as to sign a written contract before reading the fine print. We know that it only makes good sense to protect ourselves that way. Yet many times we will stake success on an interpersonal communications contract before understanding the fine print of the message. Think of *listening for false signals* as studying the fine print before you agree to the contract, and proceed accordingly.

If you proceed slowly, leaving space for clarifying responses, you can get both messages: the one that is apparently being expressed and the one that may yet need to be expressed. Stop earlier, before you've spilled all your beans, and let other people talk.

If people don't volunteer to talk, ask a question or questions that will elicit clarifying responses for you. But remember, when you start asking questions of people, you will probably get them feeling more involved, and you also then take the risk that you may not get the answers that you want from them.

Before a meeting it's always a good idea to have done some homework. Don't ask for somebody's support at a meeting unless it has been agreed to beforehand that the person is going to support you. Heads nodding in agreement and nonspecific statements and questions that only imply agreement are not reliable. They can be false signals.

No one else can tell you whether the signals you're getting are false or reliable. Your judgment will be based on how you perceive the situation you are in, the people that you're with and the *fine print* of the verbal communications. The more you listen for false signals, the more skilled you'll become at recognizing them when others send them and at intercepting your own false signals almost before you think them, and certainly before you express them.

· 10 ·
Listen for Results
(Don't Unsell What They
Have Already Bought)

People who don't understand the value of silence and who don't exercise the control to listen to it comfortably are defeating themselves. Usually they don't realize what is happening to them. They are the salespeople who can be heard saying things like, "I don't understand what happened. I was sure I had that sale made." They are the disappointed employees who say, "I was so certain that this time I had convinced him I deserved a raise." They are the parents who wonder, "Why don't my children ever listen to me when I try to give them guidance?" They are the spouses who grumble to themselves, "I don't know why I can never win an argument." They are all people who have a lack of awareness and a lack of control of *the use of silence*. Like some gamblers, they haven't yet learned how to quit while they're ahead. Instead of *using* the periods of silence that occur during any verbal transaction, conversation or, yes, even quarrel, they rush in to fill the void, going on and on with words and more words, never allowing themselves a minute to *listen for the results of what they said*.

We submit that *everyone* in business is in the business of selling, no matter what the actual job description or duties. You may not be the person who sells the company's product directly to its customers, but as a representative of that company, you are selling it indirectly. Some of the time you are selling ideas. When you make a presentation on any subject, such as ways of improving employee safety and morale, you are selling employee safety and morale. When you approach your employer to ask for a salary increase, you are selling your importance and value to him and to the company. Everybody's selling something at some time. But unless you *listen for results,* the "pitch" will go on and on. The sale may be made but be unrecognized. When there is no reason to continue selling, an "oversell" occurs. When you oversell, you usually lose the sale.

A new salesman who worked door to door selling an encyclopedia for children learned this lesson at the cost of his first sale. He had concluded his presentation to the mother of a five-year-old boy, and although he sensed that he had already convinced her of the value of the books to her son, just to make sure he went on and used one more of his highly charged sales techniques.

"If the answer to any question your little boy asks can't be found in this encyclopedia, I will refuse to sell these books to you," he said to the mother. Then, turning to the five-year-old, he said, "Ask me a question, sonny. Just ask me anything you want to know, and I'll show your mother where she can find the answer in this wonderful encyclopedia."

The five-year-old was thoughtful only a moment before he asked, "What kind of car does God drive?"

That experience was educational for the salesman. He never asked that question again, and he traded in the high-pressure sales techniques for a more listening approach.

When Cathy G. was given a well-deserved promotion with commensurate salary increase, she decided she would buy herself a new car. Cathy felt that she couldn't yet afford the luxurious car of her dreams, but she had one in mind that came close enough for now. She didn't have to look around because she had already done some comparison shopping and knew where she could get the best buy. Cathy walked into the dealership where she had spotted the car some time ago and asked the salesman who approached her, "Do you have this car in blue?" He said they did, and Cathy said, "Good. I'll buy it."

The salesman was so overwhelmed by having sold a car without even trying that he fell right into the new salesman trap and started delivering his sales pitch.

"Ms. G., it's really delightful to meet someone who knows exactly what she wants and doesn't hesitate to make a decision," he began. "You're very smart, Ms. G., to have chosen this particular model because it has every possible option on it." He kept talking, on and on, and Cathy was getting impatient. She took out her checkbook to try to bring the transaction to a close.

Then, in the middle of the sales pitch, he said, "Ms. G., did you know that our competition's luxury car, with the same options on it as this model, would cost you three hundred more?"

The car he was referring to was Cathy's dream car. "No, I didn't know that," Cathy said slowly, putting her checkbook back in her purse. What's three hundred more when I'm financing it anyway? she thought to herself as she walked out of that showroom to head for the other.

Cathy's car of her dreams is now four years old, and she's still glad she bought it. The talkative salesman lost his sale because he didn't *listen for results*. He didn't know when to stop.

It doesn't take very long at all for people to make this kind of mistake and to talk themselves right out of a contract they don't realize they have already sold. Sometimes only a word or a phrase is sufficient. Muriel P. happened to see a small sculpture that impressed her as a truly beautiful piece of art. Because it happened to be very expensive, too, Muriel hesitated, debating with herself whether she should buy it. Finally she decided affirmatively, and she told the salesman, "I'll take it."

"Fine," the salesman said. "I think you're making a wise decision. It's awfully good work, even if it isn't an original."

Until that moment Muriel hadn't realized that the sculpture was a reproduction rather than an original work. She thought to herself, Uh-oh. It's just a copy, but it's awfully expensive. I think maybe it's just too much to pay for a copy. She said to the salesman, "I've changed my mind. I don't want it after all." He had made the sale and then lost it by putting another idea into Muriel's mind, all in only a few seconds.

This sort of thing doesn't happen exclusively in the business world. We see the same thing all the time in our private lives. Wesley L. was going through the day's mail when he discovered an overdue notice from the mortgage company. He knew that meant that his wife, Paula, had forgotten to send in the payment. Forgetfulness had always been Paula's only fault in Wesley's eyes, but it created serious problems sometimes.

"Paula, I have to tell you that you are not paying enough attention to certain things, like this, and I'm very upset," Wesley said calmly.

"You're right, Wesley," Paula said contritely, "and I'm very sorry. It was very careless of me and I promise I won't let it happen again."

"You know, I don't think you fully understand how serious this is and how badly I feel," Wesley continued.

"But I really do," Paula said, "and I really am sorry. It *won't* happen again."

But Wesley was uncomfortable with the silence, and he failed to *listen for the results*.

He was about to start all over again when Paula interrupted him. "Wesley, wait a minute. You have made your point to me, I agreed with it and you got your results. But in just one more minute you're going to oversell and the pendulum is going to swing back the other way," she said very politely. "I think you'd better stop." There was silence in the room for the second time. Perhaps five or six uncomfortable seconds passed, then Wesley said, laughing, "Okay. But you're taking all the fun out of it."

There's probably at least as much good in good silence as there is in good speech. While you're building your arsenal of communication skills, practice as well the fine and valuable arts of *listening to silence* and *listening for results*. They will serve you well.

· 11 ·
The Power of Silence
(Louder Than Words)

When Tina's mother mentioned at the breakfast table that Tina's boyfriend had stayed very late last night, the young girl said, "Yes, Mother, did the noise disturb you?"

Her mother answered, "No, but the periods of silence did."

Of course they did. Listening to silence is the most intolerable thing anyone of the twentieth-century world can be asked to do. Silence has different meanings, in different situations, for each of us. Sometimes we're afraid of it. Sometimes we're intimidated by it. Sometimes, like Tina's mother, it makes us uncomfortable. But there's one thing on which we all agree: we generally just don't like it.

But silence is also fascinating and powerful. It can be one of the most valuable tools that the effective communicator can have, yet hardly any of us really use it to our benefit because most of us don't understand it. The strangest and most interesting things can happen in just a few seconds of silence.

When the great American inventor Thomas Edison

received an offer from the Western Union Company for the ticker he had invented, he was undecided as to what price to ask and requested that he be allowed a couple of days to think about it. The buyer agreed, and during that time Edison and his wife talked it over thoroughly. But he still couldn't decide on a price. Finally Mrs. Edison suggested that he ask for $20,000. Edison was stunned by the enormity of the value she placed on his invention. He thought that seemed an exorbitant figure. However, at the appointed time he returned to the Western Union office prepared to ask for that amount.

"Well, now, Mr. Edison," the Western Union representative said after he had greeted him. "How much do you want?"

But when Edison tried to say $20,000, it still seemed so outrageous a price to him that the words stuck in his mouth. He hesitated, and then he stood speechless before the Western Union official. In the quiet that followed, the official waited restlessly for Edison to answer. Still Edison did not speak.

Then the impatient businessman, unable to tolerate any more than a moment or two of silence of this nature, broke the silence. What he said was, "How about a hundred thousand dollars?"

Clearly it was Edison who benefited from that silence and the Western Union Company that lost, because its representative lacked the *control* to *listen to silence*.

People in business have a tendency to say what they want to say without having the control to wait and listen to the silence until the other person can come out with his statement. We prefer to bring business transactions to their conclusion as expeditiously as possible. Listening to silence takes some control; many people simply can't stand just to be quiet, waiting patiently, tolerating the silence long enough for the inevitable results to happen.

If you have just finished talking and are waiting for a reaction, but all you get is silence, that silence has a very definite meaning. Silence generally means one of three things: (1) your listener is taking time to digest what you just said; (2) your listener does not quite understand what you just said; or (3) your listener has reacted negatively to what you just said. The main point to remember is that if you break the silence first, you have lost control. *Don't,* even though a minute of silence may seem like an eternity.

People digest what they hear at different rates of speed. Sometimes someone will grasp what you have said very quickly; at other times that same person will really have to ponder it. When someone doesn't answer you immediately, during that silence he may be seriously considering what you said, letting it register fully, and perhaps figuring out whether he has a question and what that question is. Or maybe he didn't understand what you said, and is thinking about how to tell you he didn't understand. If you allow him the time to communicate that information to you at his own speed, then you will also have given yourself an opportunity to explain what you said in another way so you will be understood.

If someone disagrees with what you have said, silence will allow him to tell you how and why he disagrees with you. But if you go right on talking, that person will be forced to swallow his disagreement. It will still be there just the same after you have left the room. But silence allows it to be *verbalized.*

When the silence means that the other person is feeling negative about what you have just said, you can be sure it's uncomfortable for him. He will try to bridge the gap if you allow him the time. He will try to give you the reason he is negative. That reason may well be something you can counter and, by doing so, change his mind. By being quiet, you're letting the other person have time to think, to comment, to react.

An example of this was Peter R.'s trip to the dentist to have a gold crown put on one of his teeth. As he was working, the dentist looked at the tooth next to the one getting the gold crown. It had a silver filling.

"While you're here, Peter, you really should let me take the silver filling out of this tooth and put on another gold crown," the dentist said. "That silver fill-ing's not going to last long, and you can avoid going through this all over again."

There was a silence, part of the time because the den-tist's hand was in Peter's mouth. But during that silence Peter was thinking, running the information through his mind. His thoughts were, Gosh, another gold crown. That's over three hundred dollars. I really don't want to spend that much more money right now. But he's right. If I'm going to have to come back in here in another two or three months for another gold crown, I might as well have it done now. After all, my time is worth some-thing. And going through all this pain and discomfort again isn't something I exactly want to look forward to. I guess I'll let him go ahead and do it while I'm here.

While Peter was thinking those thoughts, making his decision, the dentist was getting uncomfortable with the silence. He picked up a tool and began examining the silver filling. Then he started to talk, putting sound into the silence.

"Hmm. This is really in pretty solid," the dentist commented. "Surprising. Whoever put that filling in there really put it in to stay."

"Well, then, I think I'll just leave it there for now," Peter said, reacting to the new information. The dentist argued with Peter the rest of the time he was there, but he didn't change Peter's mind.

The dentist had already made the sale, although he didn't know it. Because he was uncomfortable with the silence and didn't wait for the other person to break it, he lost control—and the sale—all in a period of two minutes!

The comedian Jack Benny used silence magnificently. In one of his running gags he was confronted by an armed robber who said, "Your money or your life." There would be a full ten-second silence. Few enter-tainers have ever had the *control* that he did, enabling him just to stand on the stage and wait for the laughter, but the audience would crack up every time. Then, even as the laughter was dying down, he would remain in control—he would wait again, and he would get yet another laugh.

Finally, the robber would repeat, "Hey, mister, I said your money or your life!" Jack would reply, "I'm thinking. I'm thinking." And the audience would roar again.

Being quiet is actually a very mature aspect of good verbal communications. But although it sounds quite logical, people tend not to do it. Instead they insist on filling up the silence. That, however, is precisely what makes silence such a powerful tool for those who have the control to use it: other people will want to fill the gap of silence when you don't. It becomes a question of who blinks first.

Lorraine J.'s employers had only recently occupied a suite of rooms in a new office complex when Lorraine noticed that there were two large scratches across the picture window that overlooked an atrium. Lorraine sent word to the building manager that there was a problem, and he came to see what it was.

As she showed him the scratches in the picture window, she said, "Isn't that a shame? Those scratches are interfering with our beautiful view of the atrium, which is the reason we chose these offices."

"It sure is a shame," the building manager agreed, "and I'm going to speak to the window cleaners about that because I certainly don't want that to happen again. But of course I can't do anything about this window now."

Lorraine said nothing for four or five seconds.

"Well, what did you want me to do about it?" he asked.

"What can you do?" Lorraine said quietly.

"There isn't anything I can do about it," he repeated. "It's just the way it is. Things like that happen. There isn't anything I can do about it!"

Lorraine just looked at him.

"You don't really mean to tell me that you expect me to replace that window, do you?" he said indignantly. "Why, they cost a hundred and fifty dollars apiece.

This is a beautiful building, everything else is fine, and what're two little scratches? They don't mean a thing. People will look right past those scratches."

Lorraine only smiled.

Two weeks later she had a new window.

A lot of people would have been too impatient to do what Lorraine did. They would have insisted, "What are you going to do about it?" But Lorraine listened to the silence and used it to get exactly what she wanted without getting into an argument that she might have lost. Lorraine's silence made the building manager so uncomfortable that he kept talking, saying more and more, building it up all by himself. Lorraine had control of the situation because she was silent, not letting it turn into a disagreeable yes-you-should no-I-shouldn't dispute. But she also was careful not to back the building manager into a corner where he would refuse to do something that he really didn't want to do.

Lorraine understand how silence works and how to make it work for her. Her rule is that knowing when to be quiet is at least as important as knowing when to speak out. She wishes everyone could learn to listen to silence, too. She says, "After all, I've never lost face by keeping the lower half of it shut."

· 12 ·
Look for Clues
to Other People's Moods
(Uncommon Sense)

David A. was the regional sales manager for Southwest Aptech-Rease Corporation (SARC). When the company made plans to expand its territory to include the Midwest, the vice-president in charge of sales told David that he wanted him to open up that area for them.

The executives at SARC were convinced that if they could get a contract with Clover-Famrods, a Chicago firm with a reputation for conservatism in business, it would open the door to the Midwest for them. David made an appointment with the head of sales at Clover-Famrods and then spent the next six weeks in conferences and meetings and researching the Chicago firm, painstakingly putting together his presentation. Then on the appointed day he flew to Chicago for his meeting with his counterpart at Clover-Famrods.

When his flight arrived right on time and a car was ready and waiting to take him to Clover-Famrods, David felt confident that everything would go smoothly. When he got to the other man's office, however, he was kept waiting forty-five minutes before being shown in. Then, as David entered the office, he got his second sense of something not being quite right. The sales manager was talking on the telephone, and as David entered the room, he heard him impatiently trying to conclude the conversation.

"Yes . . . Yes . . . All right . . . Just do whatever you have to do . . . Yes, I agree . . . Yes, do whatever you can there, and I'll see if I can pull something together here." Then he slammed the telephone down loudly and turned to face David.

That was when David saw that the man's shirt collar was unbuttoned and his necktie was askew. In contrast to the neatness of the room, his desk was in total disarray, piled high with papers.

"Sorry to keep you waiting . . . uh . . . David, isn't it?" he said with a voice that still had a tone of irritation in it.

"That's quite all right," David said. "I'm glad we could get together." But even as he spoke, David was aware that the other man was not returning his eye contact. In fact, his eyes were darting distractedly around the room while his fingers drummed nervously on the edge of the desk. Finally, with a weary sigh, he leaned back in his chair and folded his arms tightly across his chest.

"Okay, let's get started," he said.

"You know, it looks like you've had some unexpected business matters come up today," David said. "I don't think this is really the right time for us to try to talk. I believe that I would rather come back another time."

"What are you talking about?" the other man challenged in a loud voice. "You just traveled almost two thousand miles to keep this appointment. It's ridiculous for you to spend all that time and money and come this far for nothing at all. Come on, let's talk about it right now."

"I've got your call to New York on line one, and Smithers is holding on line two," the secretary's voice came over the intercom.

"I can see that you're besieged from all sides, and

you've got some more important things that need your attention right now," David said. "I'll come back to talk to you at a better time." Then before the other man could protest again, David *took control* and continued, "Would you take a look at your calendar, see when you think this will all be over with, and I'll make another appointment through your secretary to come back then. You can give me the same amount of time that you were planning to give me today, and then you and I can even go out to lunch."

The other man agreed, they made another appointment and David went home.

The next day it took some courage for him to tell his boss, "He wasn't in the right frame of mind. I didn't think it was the right time. He was putting out fires. He was distracted. He wasn't ready for me. In the mood that he was in, I could never have closed the deal."

A month later David went back to Chicago. He was again shown into the office of the regional sales manager of Clover-Famrods. But this time he saw a relaxed, neatly attired businessman who cordially received him and gave him his full attention. David made the presentation, and afterward the two men went out to lunch to celebrate the consummation of the deal between their companies.

David is still considered one of the most effective people in middle management at SARC because he has the sensitivity to know when the time is right—or not right—and the courage and tact to change the scenario when he has to.

The clues that David picked up on that told him the man he had come to see was not in a receptive mood were both verbal and nonverbal. The verbal clues were the man's loud voice, his abrupt speech pattern and his weary sigh before telling David to begin. The nonverbal clues were his lateness for their appointment, his disheveled clothing and his messy desk. He leaned back in his chair, away from David, and folded his arms tightly. Taken all together, these clues painted a picture for David that he couldn't ignore.

There are always possibilities for erroneous observation. That eyewitnesses to a crime often describe conflicting details is convincing evidence that no two people see the same thing precisely the same way. It was possible that, not ever having met this man before, David was misreading the signals. But, believing that discretion really is the better part of valor, David played it safe by addressing his remarks to the obvious on which they could agree. If he had chosen to say, for example, "I can see you're in a terrible mood" instead of "I can see you're besieged," the other man could have easily responded with, "Who do you think you are to tell me what mood I'm in?" He might have been just protecting his privacy, because after all, everyone has the right to choose with whom to share feelings. Or he might have been responding to his bad mood, unconsciously confirming David's observation, although David could have taken small comfort from that.

Since his instincts told him that, right or wrong, this was not a favorable environment in which to make a presentation, he decided to try to back off from the situation. Backing away gracefully is never easy and requires a great deal of tact, but it was the wisest choice. David felt that under the circumstances, he had nothing to lose by postponing the discussion. As it worked out, he had very much more to gain. Being able to wait for a better time to ask for what you want is just good business sense.

Parents know that there is such a thing as the right time to talk to their children to gain their cooperation. When eight-year-old Eddie comes home early from a friend's house with a slow, dragging step and doesn't go straight to the refrigerator as usual, his parents get the signal that something is awry. The message is that something is bothering him, and he may need some help to talk about it. This is not the time for them to ask him when he's going to clean up his room.

People who spend a lot of time together, such as spouses and family members, usually become fairly knowledgeable about the clues to the moods of the others. Sometimes close friends or people who have known each other for a long time become intuitive about each other's moods.

All of us, all the time, can sense other people's moods and base our decisions on what we sense, either consciously or unconsciously. And a good deal of the time we are right. But watch out for that old self-set trap: making an assumption. Warren D. told us how he had been dramatically made aware of that human-relations error. Warren had been working with Charlie for over eighteen months in the accounting department of Permaworth and Dunstorn, and he felt that he and Charlie had pretty good rapport. They often worked closely on different programs, ate lunch together at least once a week and were both on the company bowling team. A couple of times when they had had a few minutes for a break, they had sat in Charlie's office and chatted. Charlie liked to tell jokes, Warren enjoyed hearing them, and they'd have a few laughs together. To Warren, Charlie was a good-natured guy, and Warren really liked him.

That was why Warren felt completely comfortable about just walking into Charlie's office one morning and saying, "Hey, Charlie, where were you yesterday when we all went to lunch together?"

Charlie looked up and in a cold voice said, "What business is it of yours?"

Warren was startled and more than a little confused. He thought his question was innocuous, but it had really set that sweet, good-natured Charlie on edge. He couldn't figure out what had happened. "Sorry," he mumbled and hurried away.

Later that day Charlie walked into Warren's office and apologized. "You just hit me at a terrible time," he explained. "I was getting ready to go to lunch yesterday when a phone call came from the police that my son had wrecked his motorcycle and was in the emergency room at the hospital. They had to admit him, and I sat up all night waiting until I was sure he was okay before I left. I went home, cleaned up, changed my clothes and came straight to work without getting any rest. Then just before you came in, my wife called to tell me that my prizewinning black Labrador, which I raised from a pup, had gotten out of the yard and was nowhere in sight. I was mad at the world." After a few moments Charlie looked up, shrugged and grinned. "What can you do?" he quipped. "That's life, isn't it?" He was almost his old self again.

"I owe you an apology, too," Warren said. "I shouldn't have just come on the way I did."

What Warren had said didn't get him into terrible trouble. Charlie and Warren's relationship was undamaged. But Warren thought it over and learned a valuable lesson from it. He decided that from then on he would not take his relationships with others so casually. He realized that if he was going to continue to get along with people and gain their cooperation, he must not take their moods for granted. Every person, even the most stable and even-tempered, has bad days. From then on, instead of assuming that he *knew* how the other person would react, Warren started testing the water for that person's mood. He had always known that if the comptroller was in a bad mood, it was not the time to talk to him about a change in the budget. That was just common sense. But he had never before thought of determining the mood of people he felt closer to as well.

Your first impression of a person's moods can be very deceiving, because some people are better at covering up their feelings than others. But you can still learn a lot about what to expect when you walk into a person's office if you heighten your awareness and sensitivity, as Warren did, of both the verbal and nonverbal messages. One without the other could be a distortion, but taken together, they can give you valuable insight into mood. This awareness can be another key to the control you want for handling situations in both your business and private lives.

Physical reactions are difficult for any of us to hide and are usually good clues to mood. For example, tension can cause us to get sweaty palms. Embarrassment can make us blush. In very uncomfortable situations some people will begin to tremble, mostly in their hands or legs. They may try to cover it up by keeping their hands in their pockets or by crossing their legs. But if your instincts tell you what is happening, you might try to postpone dealing with the situation as gracefully as possible. You don't want to try to get feedback on your new record-keeping system from someone who is so distracted by tension. On the other hand, if you are the interviewer you might want to try to help the person be more at ease.

But remember to listen very carefully to what the other person is saying as you note that he is perspiring or trembling. The correct message will be a combination of all the clues.

You probably have heard the old saying, It's not what you say, it's how you say it. A good clue to the real meaning of what's being said is in the sound of the voice. There are many voice clues you can listen for. Really listen on a conscious level for things like tone of voice, pitch, loudness or softness and the way they affect the meaning of what you hear someone saying.

There are certain voice sounds we have become so used to hearing that we have come to expect them. They are standards in our verbal communications. For example, we expect someone's voice to go up at the end of a question, as when asking "What did you say?" or "How do you like your new job?" We expect the voice to go down at the end of a statement, such as "I enjoyed this book" or "I always do that." If the voice doesn't match what is being said, we always notice it.

You may have seen a performance by a comedian named Pat Paulsen. During political campaigns he spoofs candidates by erasing all animation from his voice and face while he delivers outrageous commentaries as if they were serious political campaign speeches. The mixed clues he sends out are bewildering to the audience at first, but then as everyone realizes what is happening, it becomes hilariously funny.

Another comedy routine also demonstrates this. The

comedian speaks in French, reciting something absurd, like a menu or instructions for putting a bicycle together, but he uses a tone of voice and a cadence that are unmistakably sensual. The audience always laughs when they find out what the words actually mean.

But mixing clues is really only funny onstage. Carrying such behavior into the real world of business would thoroughly bewilder a person's associates, and they wouldn't think it at all funny. At a meeting this person might merely be presenting his ideas, but the mood implied by an excited voice and a flushed face would convey the message that he was fighting for his ideas. Conversely, a person who is fighting for his ideas with very little facial expression and a flat, low voice would give the impression that it was really a matter of indifference to him. These people might be doing this consciously, or they might not even be aware that they are doing it, but they will eventually destroy any confidence their associates have in them.

Some people, often just from bad habit, send out faulty mood messages by speaking in a flat, expressionless voice when they do not feel that way at all. Most of us have known someone who always sounds bright and cheerful even when he is actually miserable and suffering. We may admire such a person's stoicism, but these people make it very difficult for others around them to be sensitive to their moods or considerate of their feelings.

When we send out these *mixed clues*, confusing others who have to deal with us, it only raises unintentional questions in their minds: just what did he mean by that? Why was she smiling when she told us that terrible news? Was that sarcasm or irony or nervousness?

As you practice listening to learn about the other person's mood, and as you begin to understand and monitor mood messages more skillfully, you will also begin to understand and monitor your own. Being aware of your own messages is no less important than being aware of the other person's messages. Being in a certain mood will not only broadcast something to others around you but will color the way you see others. It bears repeating here that communications work on the act/react principle. Just as the moods of others affect your decisions, your moods will affect their decisions.

You can—and you should—go beyond the voice and words by listening to the way something is said. The *body language* of the person who is speaking also communicates a lot, coloring what we hear. Certain body movements, like certain voice sounds, have come to be interpreted generally as having a particular meaning. For example, restless movements of the hands, like twisting a ring or tapping on a furniture surface, are usually taken as indications of nervousness. A sudden drop of the head or loss of facial expression frequently suggests feelings of guilt or sadness or having something to hide. Doodling or slumping in a seat seems to broadcast boredom. A furrowed brow indicates deep thought; a downcast expression, worry. A handshake usually communicates friendliness; a firm handshake shows strength of character. A hand on the shoulder is generally interpreted as being supportive. Then again, it could be interpreted as being domineering. Some gestures have even become clichés, such as a preacher's gesture upward when he mentions heaven and downward when he is warning of hellfire and damnation.

When you were a child did you believe that when your ear was ringing it meant someone was talking about you? Or that when your nose itched it meant you were going to have a fight? We don't know about that ringing in the ear, but psychologists who have studied body language say that when someone scratches his nose, it may really mean that he is disagreeing or questioning you. Of course, it could also just mean that his nose itches. But that's exactly why it is so important to take *all* the messages and *all* the signals into consideration. It isn't as hard to do as it might seem.

We all constantly receive, interpret and react to many messages on an unconscious level, because there are too many for us to try to handle them all consciously. All things considered, we make surprisingly few errors.

We are all also familiar with situations in which the verbal and nonverbal messages combine in one very clear message about mood. For example, we know what it means without thinking about it when someone we're talking to says, "Yes, yes, I know," and turns away. The combined message is, "I've heard enough. I understand what you said. I don't want to listen anymore. You're overselling."

You already know how to relate the verbal and nonverbal messages to the emotional states of the people you know. You do it all the time without even thinking about it. And you've learned to do it by *listening* and by *observation*, even though you may not do it on a conscious level. Now all you need to do is bring that ability up to the conscious level, where you can make it work for you, where you can begin consciously to evaluate the other person's moods. Eventually, as the process of listening to learn about the other person's mood becomes more of an automatic reaction, the appropriate approach will come to you as easily as if it were part of the unconscious process.

One other aspect of body language that we believe is worth your awareness is what psychologists call personal space. It is a very sensitive matter and a very important part of our relations with other people.

Psychologists have done studies that show that while people vary greatly in their perceptions of their own comfort zones, everyone lives within a personal space. This space is demarcated by an imaginary circle, and we all react negatively to having that zone invaded by somebody else. If you step uninvited into another person's space, he will probably send you both verbal and nonverbal messages to let you know that you have committed a transgression. The other person is very likely to become tense, irritable, even hostile, and to verbalize those feelings.

"I don't know if it's the weather or the terrible world tensions," Harry T. complained to a friend over lunch one day. "I think I'm a good salesman and a good judge of people, but it's really hard for me to understand some of my customers. Take this morning, for instance. I made my presentation, and the customer was smiling and nodding his head, so I was sure we had a deal. When he finally said yes, I went around his desk, pulled up a chair and started laying out the papers. Just like that his smile disappeared, he frowned, pushed his chair back and stood up. Then he said, 'Well, just leave it with me, and I'll let you know what I decide.' I don't get it. What a moody guy!''

Harry was insensitive to his customer's discomfort at having his personal space invaded. He wasn't aware of the way one false move can drown out the best sales talk. Maybe Harry's other customers are not as sensitive as this man, but if Harry doesn't learn to respect personal space and test for each person's imaginary circle, he may lose other sales because of it.

People will let you know verbally and nonverbally if you cross that imaginary personal-space line. You should be sensitive to that. Don't invade; but if you should do so inadvertently, listen for the message and step back.

It can be helpful for you to become aware of what you do with personal space. Most families have clearly defined private areas, but do you know how you manage space in your business setting? For example, do you dominate your supervisors or co-workers by bending too closely over them at their desks? Do you stand too close to people when you are talking to them, making them uncomfortable, or do you keep an appropriate distance? Do you resent someone reading over your shoulder, or know others who do? Do you always sit in the back of the meeting room, missing some of what's going on? Do you pull your chair up to the conference table or set it safely in the corner? Are you deferring to others out of courtesy, or is it that you prefer to be inconspicuous? Which message are you sending to the people around you? Is it the one you *want* to send?

The significance of body language is evident everywhere. In our literature physical description is used to reveal mood. For example, bowed shoulders indicate someone dealing with a heavy emotional load, even defeat, while squared shoulders indicate someone who is ready to take on responsibility. Body language is also evident in the way it is used by actors, politicians, talk-show hosts and every other kind of public figure. For example, if someone wants to appear "cool" or completely in control of his emotions, he will probably have little or no vocal or facial animation, à la James Bond.

In summary: observing indications of others' moods is helpful if you keep in mind that there is always the potential for confusion. First of all, identify to yourself exactly what you observe of someone's verbal and non-verbal clues, without passing judgment too quickly. Consider all the possibilities. That yawn might mean merely that he didn't sleep well last night. That pained look could also mean he has a headache. He could be laughing with you, not at you. Be sure your observations are accurate, then act on them, making a decision, not a superficial judgment. It isn't always easy, but it's definitely worth the effort.

Be sure your own facial expressions, your eye contact and your stance are telling the other person, "I'm really paying attention to you. I want to hear everything you say." Remember that moods change. They should be actively searched out and consciously dealt with, because you don't live in the world by yourself. You must find ways to make adjustments within yourself.

Listening to learn the mood of the other person is an important part of making that inner adjustment. Other people will send you the messages, and you will receive them without even trying. But the *approach* has to come from you, because what you do with the messages after you receive them is up to you.

·13·
Find the "Hotbutton"
(To Gain Access,
Press Button)

The younger man, having won the heart of the girl he loved, now had to ask her father's consent for them to marry. Forearmed with the knowledge of the reputation his future father-in-law had for being a tightwad, the astute young man opened the interview with, "Sir, I know a way by which you can save a lot of money."

He got the girl, of course, because he had hit her father's "hotbutton." He knew what that man wanted. And he probably lived happily ever after, because anyone who is that skilled at finding and using the hotbuttons of others is certain to succeed in business and make friends everywhere he goes.

Whether or not you believe the story, you should have no doubts about the importance of hotbuttons. We all have hotbuttons that turn us on or off, and everyone reacts to them, consciously or unconsciously. Whether or not people recognize their own hotbuttons, if *you* know what they are and use them well, you too will speak the language of success.

Some hotbuttons are just human nature. These are things we know will elicit a certain response from most people in a given situation. An example of this appeared in a newspaper advice column. A woman wrote a letter asking, "How can I get my husband to discuss business affairs with me?" The answer was, "Ask him when he intends to buy a new car." Money is a common hotbutton, and thus that might very well open up a spirited discussion of finances. But we should not assume that everyone will always be turned on or off, for better or worse, by the same things.

Some people want wealth, some want recognition, others want to be thought of as philanthropists, or as warm, or friendly, or creative in business. People want so many different things that the list is almost limitless. Despite that, you should be able to find out what hotbuttons other people have. You don't have to be a psychologist; you only need a little understanding of human behavior.

Benjamin Franklin had that understanding of human psychology at a time when there was no such professional discipline. He knew how to influence people in order to win them to his side by appealing to their special interests. Franklin was newly elected to a political position in Pennsylvania, but during the campaign he had unexpectedly made an enemy of a man whose support he felt he needed. Knowing that this man owned a collection of books that included one particularly rare volume, Franklin sent a note to the man asking "a great favor." Would it be possible for Franklin to borrow the book for a few days?

A messenger delivered the book almost immediately, and Franklin returned it one week later with another note expressing his gratitude. The result was that when they next met, the other man spoke to Franklin for the first time and with civility expressed his readiness to cooperate in any way he could. Their friendship continued until the other man's death.

Franklin had recognized that this man's special interest was his fine library, of which he was very proud. The rare book was the hotbutton, and Franklin's expressed appreciation for it brought the two men together. If

Franklin had approached this important man in any other way, he would probably have gained nothing.

William Norris is the founder and president of Control Data Corporation. He has all the characteristics we generally associate with the highly successful person. But there is something else Mr. Norris wants: he wants to be remembered for making a humanitarian mark on the world through helping people of the inner cities. He is interested in human development, education and economic progress for people who have very little opportunity to come into the mainstream. He builds factories, trains people to work in them and even puts in childcare facilities so working mothers know their children are in good hands while they're at work. He underwrites people who want to start their own businesses, and he makes it possible for them to get loans.

You probably would be safe in assuming that anyone who wants access to Mr. Norris with something to sell him would do well to point it toward human development. That's his special interest, his hotbutton.

People of modest means have been known to reject money as a hotbutton. Robert E. Lee was approached at the close of the Civil War by a representative of a large insurance company, who offered Lee the presidency of the firm at a salary of $50,000 a year. One of Lee's priorities at the time was to earn a living, but he had to state honestly that he seriously doubted that his services were worth quite so generous a sum.

"We aren't interested in your services," the man said. "We only want your name."

"That," Lee said quietly but firmly, "is not for sale."

Lee later accepted a position as the president of a college at a salary of $1,500 a year.

That insurance company representative hadn't done his homework before approaching Lee. Had he done so, he would have realized that a man who was known for placing a high value on honor would never agree to sell his name for any amount of money. The insurance executive actually hit a *negative* hotbutton and lost his case, along with any hope of ever redeeming it.

A young friend of ours who holds a Ph.D. in mathematics and computer technology was very happily employed at a large electronics manufacturing corporation in Texas. His qualifications kept him very much in demand, and he was frequently approached for recruitment by other national corporations. Most recently he was contacted by a large East Coast company and invited to come for an interview.

"There's really no way I would want to go to work for them," he said at first. "I don't want to live in New York or New Jersey. I really like the Southwest." But they persisted, and he finally agreed to go East for an interview. "I love to travel," he said, "so if they want to pay for me to make a trip up there to talk to them, I'll do it."

He went to New Jersey and was shown around and introduced to everyone, and that night the head of the department took him out to dinner. They were just making conversation, but the executive was *listening* when he learned that our young friend had a hotbutton.

The next day, when he was offering him the job, the executive said, "By the way, we have plants in Rome, Paris and London. Now, it isn't mandatory, but we would like you to check out these facilities once in a while, say about once a year." Our friend had accepted the job and returned to Dallas before he realized that he didn't even know what they would be paying him! That's the sort of thing that can happen when you listen, learn and hit the hotbutton.

The same principle also applies to everyday relations with friends and family members, with the same kind of results. Janet D.'s son Kerry had become more difficult to talk to after reaching adolescence, and Janet decided to try to reach him through his hotbutton. She had become aware that thirteen-year-old Kerry placed a lot of importance on "being mature," and Janet agreed that most of the time he was successful at behaving that way. Whenever a communications problem came up between them, Janet would say, "Kerry, you know how mature I think you are. I think we can discuss this like two adults, don't you?" Immediately Kerry would respond by wanting to live up to his hotbutton. It worked much better than saying, "You really are unreasonable. I can't discuss anything with you. Why don't you ever listen?" These are negative hotbuttons.

We all constantly use hotbuttons without realizing that we are using them or whether we are using them positively or negatively. If we hit a negative hotbutton (unfortunately it's easily done), on purpose or not, the other person is no longer receptive. We have turned off that person. We are not going to get what we want.

But if we can learn what the other person's positive hotbutton is, what turns him on, and appeal to that, we can solve a lot of problems. A little sensitivity and a lot of homework will go a long way.

· 14 ·
Listen to Yourself
(Mind Your Mouth)

When Homer T. retired after twenty-five years on the job as postmaster of the Parkerville Heights Post Office, he found himself with a lot of unfilled time on his hands. Homer decided that he would take advantage of this by pursuing a dream he had always had: he would become active in the politics of his hometown. Homer's family supported his new interest wholeheartedly.

Homer had never been much of a talker, as some of his political opponents were, so he enrolled in a public-speaking course to tilt the odds just a little more in his favor. Homer was surprised to learn that he really had a bit of a flair for oratory.

The whole family respectfully listened to Homer rehearse for hours at home, and they all went to hear him whenever he had a speaking engagement. Homer had apparently fallen in love with words. He was having such a marvelous time that he never even noticed that the turnout for his speeches were declining steadily.

Then one morning Homer was coming down the back stairs to the kitchen when he overheard Bobby talking to his father.

"Why does Grandpa act so differently now?" Bobby was asking.

"I don't think your grandpa is any different, Bobby. He's still your grandpa," his dad said. "But how do you think he has changed?"

"Well," Bobby began, then hesitated as though searching for the right words. "I guess it's that when Grandpa didn't used to talk very much, he always made a lot of sense. And now it seems like he talks all the time but he doesn't say anything."

Homer got his young grandson's message, took an honest listen to himself and made some adjustments in his speech-making technique. Unfortunately it was too late for him to salvage his election campaign.

In learning to listen to himself, sparing the words and saving the speech, Homer T. actually joined the ranks of some of this country's greatest politicians. George Washington never hesitated to talk when it was necessary or to keep his silence when it was not. Abraham Lincoln was known for his tendency to withdraw from the social chatter around him and to speak only when he thought there was a good reason for him to contribute his comments. Calvin Coolidge, who enjoyed a worldwide reputation for being laconic, never lacked for words when he had something he wanted to say. Yet Washington and Lincoln are remembered for their famous speeches, and Coolidge's pithy, straight-to-the-point observations are often quoted.

Although most of us will never have to make speeches to get elected to public office, we all have to make different but equally important speeches of a sort every day of our lives. We are making a speech every time we make a sale, voice a complaint, put a point across or defend a position, explain an action or teach a technique. Sometimes we have time to prepare, but more often it must be extemporaneous. But since we've usually done some of these things once or twice before, we have a backlog of experience to help us get through such situations.

Imagine that your supervisor has told you he is dissatisfied with a particular employee's performance. He wants you to fire him, and he wants it done today. No one likes to have to do that kind of thing, but the responsibility has been given to you, whether you like it or not.

You call the person into your office. If you've had to do this before, you remember what you learned from the other occasions. But even if you have no experience, you want to try to make it as painless as possible You begin by letting him know that there is nothing personal in what you are doing. If an explanation can be of any benefit to him, you offer one, telling him, for instance, that you think that he has certain valuable talents, but that they just aren't what the particular job requires. You wish him better luck on his next job. You offer him any of the company's services that will help him in his job search, such as the use of an office, a secretary and a telephone for a reasonable period of time. Afterward, you feel good about having done what you had to do as quickly and cleanly as possible. But before you start congratulating yourself on how skillfully you got the disagreeable deed done, take a few minutes to ask yourself a few questions about *how* you did it.

What about the tone of voice you used when you told him there was nothing personal involved? Are you sure it was that of a compassionate person? Did you *listen* to it? When you told him that you think he has talents but they just weren't right for this job, were you being honest? Or were you just trying to get off the hook? Did you *sound* as though you really meant what you were saying? When you offered him the use of the company facilities, did you offer your personal assistance to him as well in locating another job? Right now you know that *you* feel better. But did you leave your former colleague feeling hopeful or hopeless?

You can't answer insightful questions like these unless you were listening to yourself. And yet for any number of different reasons, many of us simply don't take the time to do that.

Lots of times, because we simply do not listen to

ourselves, we fail to hear ourselves *as others hear us*.

Volume has a definite effect on the people you are talking to. Your awareness of this effect on others is an important part of your verbal communications. Don't be like the mother who, after severely chastising her son, angrily asked him, "Why haven't you done what I told you to?" The boy answered, "I'm sorry, Mama, but you were shouting so loudly that I couldn't hear what you were saying!"

Remember that while turning the volume up to the right level can be very effective, a well-placed whisper can be more powerful than a cannon's roar. Maude L., the mother of five burly, brawling boys, was asked how she managed to get herself heard with all those men conversing just below a shout. "Oh, it's easy," she said. "I whisper."

You also should be that careful, that thoughtful and that aware of how you are using volume. Don't restrict yourself to one volume, but don't switch around without purpose, so that you lose impact.

When you change volume, do it for a reason. Keep in *control*. Change the volume because you have been listening to yourself and wish to alter your message.

The speed at which we speak is often determined by cultural or regional influences as much as by force of habit. For example, Easterners are generally characterized as being rapid-fire talkers and Southerners as being slow drawlers. But there are also other factors that affect our rate of speech. Being excited or nervous will often put an unintended push behind our words, and being tired or bored will often slow us down. Try to control this, since it will affect the people to whom you are talking and can alter the meaning of what you are saying.

One bad habit can lead to another. If you indulge one habit, such as talking too fast, you could unconsciously find yourself falling into some other bad habits, such as finishing sentences for others. If you talk too slowly, you may have trouble finding an opportunity to say what's on your mind. The too-slow talker may also find himself lagging behind his audience, while the too-fast talker may find that his audience can't keep up with him. Neither of them will be getting his message across.

The actor John Wayne once said that he believed his talent actually lay in the distinctive way he used a pause in the middle of each sentence. It would be hard to overestimate the power of the pause in speech. But equally important is its timing.

Some pauses between words and sentences are called *dramatic* because they add emphasis to what has been said. But that same dramatic pause, held a bit too long, can begin to sound more like exaggeration or lack of self-confidence, or as if the speaker has lost his place. Pause just a little longer than that and you may lose your audience's attention completely. The well-timed short pause can suggest that you are a well-organized person who really knows what he is talking about, but the poorly timed or too-short pause can communicate that you are poorly organized and uncertain of what you are saying.

Listen to your timing. The difference isn't difficult to hear, but you do have to listen to yourself to know if it's right.

Wilson G. had been working in the Research Division of Metacomm Systems for three years and had been instrumental in the development of Metacomm's new FSR2 radar component. In his capacity as a research engineer, Wilson had gained the respect of his colleagues for his technical expertise, and he was also very well accepted because of his ability to get along so well with others. He was what people generally refer to as a nice guy. So when the time came to put together a proposal team to sell the FSR2 to the United States government, the decision was to make Wilson the proposal team manager.

On the first day of meetings, Wilson's team met with the team from Metacomm's Albur City branch office and the customer representatives from Washington. Wilson opened the meeting, speaking the same way he always had at Metacomm.

"Um . . . This is the . . . uh . . . first meeting of . . . the . . . uh . . . FSR2 . . . proposal . . . group . . . and . . . I'd like you all . . . to meet the . . . uh . . . government team that . . . is . . . uh . . . here to . . ."

Jason Y. cut in. "Before we get into all that," he said quickly, "I think we should consider moving the meetings to Albur City, because the entire FSR2 program is going to be located there eventually anyway and so it only makes good sense that we do it right now at the outset."

Wilson listened politely until Jason finished, then attempted to bring the group's attention back to the subject. But each time Wilson tried to do that, Jason interrupted and changed the subject. Wilson continued to speak very slowly and very deliberately, and so softly that some of the people in the room had to strain just to hear him. His pauses, which sounded intellectual in the lab, were too long in the meeting room, making his thoughts sound broken up and disorganized. As Wilson continued to address the group in his halting manner, Jason continued to interrupt him during those long pauses with a loud voice and rapid-fire speech. The customer representatives watched silently while the maneuvers for control went on.

When it became apparent that Wilson had completely lost control, he was relieved as proposal team manager and a new manager was assigned. Donna C. walked into the meeting room, making eye contact with everyone at the table as she shook each person's hand and said, in a firm voice, "I am the new proposal manager." She was prepared, her questions had been thought out, her voice had no hesitancy or inappropriate pauses. Her manner of speaking was clear, direct and assertive. In short, there was no doubt that she was in charge. The group was able to conclude their real business, which was to sign a contract with the government within a reasonable time.

No one would seriously argue against the importance of vocabulary in communications; of having available just the right word that most clearly expresses one's meaning. However, there is one particular group of words that can be an unexpectedly sharp double-edged sword.

The use of slang words or jargon can be an interesting or amusing verbal bridge if you really know whom you are talking to, what you are saying and why you are saying it. Slang, jargon and colloquial expressions that are not known to the person or group will not be understood. If the expressions have gone out of vogue—and they do go quickly—the speaker sounds silly.

Another good reason to avoid using these words and phrases is that so many of them are also emotion-packed. The president of a nationally known advertising agency proudly reported at an annual shareholders' meeting that ten percent of the vice-presidents in the agency were women.

"We still have a long way to go," he admitted, "but we are making progress, girls."

"Girls?" a woman's voice echoed from the audience.

If the expressions are used as a verbal shortcut, as a substitute for giving a fuller explanation, the audience might just get the impression that the speaker either hasn't prepared well or lacks sufficient command of the vocabulary.

Suffice it to say, then, that the use of slang, jargon and colloquialisms, if it is accurate and appropriate, can have a positive effect, but the potential for making yourself sound foolish is also there. Handle them with care.

In the same way, what may sound pleasant to one person can be very unpleasant to another. You may intend something as a compliment, but somehow it comes out sounding like an insult or sarcasm. If that happens to you, take comfort in the fact that you are not alone! It happens all the time. For example, Gary N. met a female acquaintance on the street one day and said to her, "Pamela, you look absolutely great!"

"Why, thank you," Pamela said, smiling warmly.

"I really mean it," Gary said, overselling. "Why, I didn't recognize you!"

Gary should have quit when he was ahead. Pamela just laughed and took the compliment as meaning that her new hairdo was a dramatic change. But sometimes, because of someone's oversensitivity, the intended compliment is taken quite literally and the more sensitive person will walk away angry and wondering, Just what did he think I looked like the last time he saw me?

The human mind seems to have an infinite capacity for tripping over its own thoughts on the way to the mouth. There are indications that it starts very early in life, as Matthew R. learned.

Matthew R. had been enrolled by his parents in Miss Maple's Academy of the Social Graces for Young Ladies and Gentlemen and was attending his first weekly tea dance. All the young ladies were wearing their frilliest dresses and little white gloves, and every young gentleman was wearing a jacket and a tie. Miss Maple was insistent that every young gentleman ask a young lady to dance.

"And remember to pay your young lady a lovely compliment," she reminded them. Matthew was having a particularly difficult time trying to think of something nice to say to his dance partner. Finally, after some mental struggling but obviously quite pleased with himself, Matthew said, "You know what, Cheryl? You dance pretty good for such a fat girl."

Usually other people hear our fluffs before we do, and usually they are amused by them. The worst pain inflicted, then, is by us on ourselves as we blush and stammer and try to explain, "Oh, but what I really meant to say was . . ." Sometimes, by trying to explain, we only dig ourselves in deeper.

Bryce W. had just concluded a report to the capitalization steering committee and was now ready to add his personal observation.

"Now I have something of real importance I want to say," Bryce began.

"That is, of course, I didn't mean to imply that what I said previously was not important; only that the point I am about to make now is *very* important. . . . That is, what I have just told you is *also* very important, but the point I wish to make now is . . ." By that time the committee members were all laughing. Bryce joined them. Then he started all over again and got it right.

A sense of humor, especially about yourself, is a saving grace. You won't get through some days, let alone an entire lifetime, if you can't see some humor in the well-intentioned errors that you and others around you are destined, by your humanness, to make. You take a risk every time you open your mouth to speak. Being prepared is important because it can spare you a lot of failure and embarrassment. But listening to yourself will not only help you avoid mistakes, it will also let you hear the slipups in time to correct them.

Sometimes they can't be fixed and the reality is that we're stuck with what we said. That's what happened to Norman W. when, because he wasn't listening to himself, he talked himself in right over his head.

Norman had made an application for a position and was being interviewed by the personnel manager. When he was told that the company had group insurance for their employees but that each employee paid for his own coverage and that it was deducted from the first paycheck of each month, Norman looked very disappointed. Noting his disappointment, the interviewer asked Norman if that presented a problem.

"At my last place of employment, the company paid for everything," he said. "They paid for our life insurance, dental insurance, health insurance, three weeks' paid vacation, a Christmas bonus, a recreational program and unlimited sick leave."

"I can't imagine why you would leave such a generous employer," the personnel man said.

There was a moment of silence before Norman realized what he had said and answered sheepishly, "They went bankrupt." It was too late to try to take that back, but Norman and the interviewer got a good laugh out of it.

Of course, if you realize your slip at once, you have the advantage, and the choice to do something.

You have about fifteen billion brain cells that work

with the speed and efficiency of a microprocessor. Run that goof back through your cerebral computer and in no more than a cool, calm split-second you can come up with a much better way to say what you meant to say but somehow didn't.

Listen to what you say. Hear it the way others hear it, and try to say it right the first time. When something goes wrong—and it occasionally will no matter how careful you try to be—keep your sense of humor handy. And if your remark needs fixing, fix it with an apology and a smile.

You might make an example of the professional musicians of the world. They very rarely make a mistake in their many live performances, in spite of the unusual number of opportunities they have, because they are so well prepared. But when they do make a mistake, they continue right on, never missing a beat and keeping the audience with them right up to the very last note.

Nothing you say has to result in a case of terminal humiliation if you *listen to yourself* and keep in control.

Besides the bloopers that happen to us all, another common fault in conversation or more formal presentations is rambling. This can be a mental disturbance in some people who are totally unable to talk in a straight line, to stay on the subject or even to finish one sentence before starting the next. But assuming you don't suffer from such a mental problem, make a deliberate effort to use these rules.

1. Speak concisely.
2. Finish one thought before starting another. Stay on the main highway of that thought without getting distracted.
3. Don't repeat.

Whenever you're speaking, ask yourself if you're getting your intended message across. Ask yourself what would happen if you lowered your voice or raised it for emphasis. Ask yourself if your voice is too loud. Too soft. Too flat. Are you giving the facts you wanted to? Do those you're speaking to understand, or do you have to adjust what you're saying to them? Do your vocal inflections reflect your meaning? Are you really saying what you want to? Are you sending contradictory messages? Can you "hear" yourself, so that you really know?

We believe that you should give yourself the same considerate attention you give to others when you are listening to them. That means listening for the same clues in your own voice and your own words and being sure you are communicating to others in the same clear way you want others to communicate with you.

Listen to your own resonance, pitch, volume, rate of speed and words—all the things you listen to in others' voices. Keep that control by *listening to yourself*. Unless you do, you may never know if you're saying something wrong. Remember, you not only have a right to say it, you have a right to say it right.

· 15 ·
Don't Be Distracted by Irrelevancies (Objection: Irrelevant, Immaterial)

A young psychiatrist complained bitterly to an older colleague that he was being worn down by having to listen to all of the troubles and problems of his patients. Noticing that the senior consultant was sprightly despite his years, the young man asked with a sigh, "How on earth do you remain so youthful, sir, while listening hour after hour, day after day and year after year to all those terrible complaints, anxieties and fears?"

The older man shrugged. "Who listens?"

All of us have had to tune out people who would nearly drive us out of our minds if we really listened to them go on . . . and on . . . and on. . . .

We all know people who, if they are asked the time, will explain how to build a watch. They inundate us with irrelevancies, and by the time they get to the main point, we're not listening anymore. When you ask a queston and someone insists on telling you much more than you want to know or care to hear, listening can get awfully hard.

Irrelevancy can be as distracting as a cough in a darkened theater, and sometimes almost as contagious.

Have you ever had a verbal exchange like this with a co-worker?

He said, "I attended that meeting of the budget committee on Tuesday morning and learned that we have a lot of problems with our budget." You heard him make a mistake and started thinking to yourself, "That meeting was on Wednesday morning, not Tuesday." You were distracted by a minor detail, and you never heard the real, very important message about your department's budget problems. You got all caught up with the person's error about what day the meeting took place, even though it was of no significance.

We say things like that all the time, things that weren't what we meant to say. Totally unaware that we have said them, we go on talking. Yet we allow ourselves to be put off the mental track by an irrelevancy such as the wrong day when we hear someone else say it. Many people have the habit of riddling their communications with irrelevancies. Identifying these people is not usually a problem, but it does take a lot of thought and a lot of organization to deal with them.

You can begin by developing heightened awareness, so that when you are listening to these people you will recognize that they are giving you more information than you need. Then when you are going to a meeting with someone who does that, you can mentally prepare yourself to discard the irrelevancies you will hear.

The discarding of irrelevancies is really a kind of balancing act, because you don't want to lose inadvertently any of the significant details while sorting out the throwaways. Imagine a colander into which a pot of cooked spaghetti has been poured, and then *listen to let the irrelevant details run through*, like the cooking water, while being careful not to lose any of the spaghetti.

With that image in mind, now imagine yourself at a business meeting where a co-worker who has the habit of getting caught in irrelevancies has been asked to report on a speaker the company sent him to hear.

"I went to hear the most interesting speaker the other day," he begins. "What he had to say was very important for all of us to know. But listen, let me tell you about the wonderful luncheon I had. It was over at the Dallas Club, and I have never seen a spread like that before. It cost only $3.50 and it was last Thursday . . . no, it was last Wednesday . . . no, I'm sure it was Thursday. But listen, that meal was sensational. They had three different entrees, from fish to chicken to prime rib. And they had two different . . . no, I'm sorry, scratch that . . . they had five different entrees, including jumbo shrimp the likes of which I haven't seen since I came up from the Gulf. And they had seven salads . . . gorgeous, just gorgeous . . . and I went back and filled my plate several times. And for dessert they had strawberries Romanoff and cheesecake. I never saw anything like it. Now, the speaker said some terrific things. . . ."

Are you the person who, while listening to him, thinks, What was he doing at the Dallas Club? I've never been asked to go there. I wonder how come he got to go there and I didn't? Besides, I know it wasn't Thursday, because he and I had lunch together at Joe's Barbecue that day. I think it wasn't even Wednesday, because I know he was out of town on Wednesday. But he's right about one thing—$3.50 for a spread like that is remarkable. I really would like to go there, even if I didn't pay any attention to the speaker at all. I'd like to have a lunch like that.

If you are that listener, by the time you get your mind back on the subject, which is, of course, the only thing of real importance, you have lost at least sixty seconds of what the speaker said.

However, if you are a listener who realizes that it was Tuesday instead of Thursday, and that the lunch was great but it has no bearing on the speaker's message, and if you drop those details because your listening is organized, then you are in control and not going to be distracted by irrelevancies.

The person who overstuffs his verbal communications with all that irrelevant detail seriously handicaps himself, especially in the business world. When you walk into someone's office, you generally have only two or three minutes to catch his attention and tell him what you want to talk about. If what you say is buried in a barrage of time-consuming irrelevancies, then you have lost those all-important minutes during which you should be getting your message across. Just as important as not being distracted by irrelevant detail is that you *do not use irrelevant detail.*

According to studies, the typical conversationalist delivers 4,800 words in the course of approximately thirty conversations a day. But the average person, according to another study, devotes only sixty seconds out of every hour to full concentration on the work at hand. If that's true, the typical person studied was attentive only about sixteen minutes out of every day. Even assuming that the studies might not be totally valid or the statistics completely accurate, it still seems that there must be a lot more talking than listening. Your chances of being heard are much improved if you use the fewest possible details to convey what you want to say. The most effective speakers are those who know what they want to say, decide how they want to say it and then stick to the subject. They are the communicators who are best understood and least likely to overhear, as they walk away, "What did he say?" "I don't know."

Ralph K. thought himself to be a very considerate employer. He made no unreasonable demands, he paid good wages and he provided an excellent program of benefits. Because he did all these things, Ralph couldn't understand why he was having so much trouble attracting and keeping qualified personnel. It also seemed to Ralph that no matter how well recommended these people came to him, they never seemed to work as well as they should.

One typical morning Ralph said to his newly hired assistant, "I want to talk to you about that correspondence from Jones and Jones. Do you know I started out working for them? My first supervisor was sure tough to work for. He used to talk all around and around until you just had to almost guess what he was trying to tell you. Now Jones and Jones are opening an account with me. That's the way it goes, I guess. A lot of their people trained here and then went to work there, you know. But then they've got that recreational facility with the tennis court and jogging trail, and nowadays young people are attracted by that sort of thing. Do you think we should make something like that available here?''

They talked about the relative cost and benefits of a workout room near the cafeteria. Two weeks later Ralph confronted his assistant.

"Ruth, I thought you were going to set up a meeting with Jones and Jones," he said.

Ruth was surprised. "I don't think we discussed that," she said.

"I'm sure we did," Ralph insisted. "I distinctly remember talking to you about it. I'm afraid we've lost that account." Frowning, Ralph retreated to his office, wondering what was wrong with these young business people today. Next door, in her office, his assistant was thinking about seeking another position, maybe with Jones and Jones.

It's not surprising that some of Ralph's employees chose to leave. It's difficult to work for someone who uses distracting irrelevancies but even harder to tell someone when he is doing it.

Exercise in Spotting Irrelevancies

Some anecdotes follow with numerous irrelevancies. Read each one through, then cross out the irrelevancies you recognize. Read again to see if even more could be omitted without detracting from the stories. You may add a word or two so your deletions make sense.

Story A—Irrelevant Version

Mike Blonford is a friend of mine from the army, and we had some of the most unbelievable experiences together. He was always getting into trouble but didn't mean to. It was just that things always happened to Mike. He never made them happen, if you know what I mean. Well, when he got out of the service, we still kept up our friendship, and he went to the police academy and became a policeman. He is really perfectly suited to this, especially since he works with young kids, not exactly as a truant officer but more as a confidant and counselor. He gets out and umpires games between street gangs, and still has time to go fishing with a kid who needs some extra companionship. He and I go fishing a lot, too, and like to break away for a weekend every once in a while, and I've got a camper we use. I built it for my pickup, and it has a couple of cots and cooking stuff and is really fixed up with everything. Mike and I had planned to get away the last week in October to a place about three hundred miles away, to a farm owned by my wife's uncle. It has beautiful trees and about as nice a bass lake as I've seen. I've taken a lot of three-pound bass out of it, and last year I landed a five-and-a-half-pounder. Mike had been wanting to go with me for a solid year, and this was the week. I went by to pick him up, and he came out looking like his eyeballs had a road map printed on them. He had been up all night heading off a potential rumble between two gangs and was dead on his feet. I persuaded him to crawl into the camper part of the truck, and he was so tired he stripped down to his undershorts and climbed into bed, and I got into the front, and we took off. I figured he could get a five- or six-hour nap so we could get in some fishing when we got there. I had driven about halfway and come to the large town of Kasper, which has about three hundred people and is one of those spots on a highway that if you blink you miss it when you go through. I jerked to a stop for a traffic light, and as I found out later, Mike woke up, thought we had arrived at the lake, opened the door and got out. Just at that moment the light changed and I took off. Mike, in his undershorts, had to find the one cop in town, explain it to him (can you picture that?), and then he and the cop chased me all the way to the lake.

Does your story, now minus the irrelevancies, look something like this?

Story A—The Heart of the Matter

Mike Blonford and I go fishing a lot. One day I went to pick him up. He had been up all night and was dead on his feet. I persuaded him to crawl into the camper part of the truck, and he was so tired he stripped down to his undershorts and climbed into bed. I got into the front and we took off. When I stopped for a traffic light later, Mike woke up, thought we had arrived at the lake, opened the door and got out. The light changed and I took off. Mike, in his undershorts, had to find the one cop in town and explain it to him, and then he and the cop chased me to the lake.

Now try your skill at spotting and eliminating the irrelevant details in this next story.

Story B—Irrelevant Version

My neighbor, Georgia Fleming, is one of those people who always seems to have a project going on, whether it's painting her house singlehanded, knitting a dress, framing pictures, making crewel seat covers for eight dining-room chairs or making chess sets out of screws and nuts and bolts. She is an avid collector of cows. She has figures of cows carved from ivory, jade, amethyst, wood, marble; figures of cows created from balloons, steel, fur, felt and plastic. She has pictures of cows and pillows of cows, and these things range from very small to absolutely enormous. There is very little room for much else in her house, and Georgia confesses that although it may be carried to excess, this hobby gives her great satisfaction. She doesn't really understand why she is fascinated with cows, except that she always wanted one when she was a child in New York City, for they looked so placid and soft in the picture books. She even tried to buy Elsie, the Borden cow, complete with Elmer, Elmo and plastic grass, but the company wouldn't sell. Besides, her husband said she absolutely couldn't keep a live cow in their yard, and since the city code doesn't allow it on quarter-acre lots, she compromised by raising white mice. One is a particular pet named Socrates. She also owns a brown-and-black alley cat named Tippy. Last Tuesday at two o'clock in the afternoon Georgia was baking an apple pie (another of her hobbies, and she is an excellent cook) when Socrates got out of his cage. Tippy spied him and began giving chase. Just then the telephone rang, and Georgia can't resist answering a ringing phone. There are people like that who just can't let a phone ring. Is that another type of compulsion, too? I once knew a woman who got out of the tub six times in a row to answer the same wrong number and says she hated herself for it but couldn't help herself. So Georgia answered the phone very excitedly and explained, "I can't talk now, our white mouse is loose and I have to catch him before the cat does." She let the receiver dangle from the hook for a good ten minutes while she chased all over the house. She finally caught the mouse and got it back into its cage. Then she ran back to the phone, only to hear an unfamiliar voice on the other end say, "Excuse me, lady, I know I have the wrong number, but I just had to find out—who got the mouse?"

How does your story compare to this one?

Story B—The Heart of the Matter

My neighbor raises mice. She also owns an alley cat. One day a mouse got out of his cage. The cat spied him and began giving chase. Just then the phone rang. My neighbor answered it very excitedly and explained, "I can't talk now, our white mouse is loose and I have to catch him before the cat does." She let the receiver dangle from the hook for a good ten minutes while she chased all over the house. She finally caught the mouse and got it back into its cage. Then she ran back to the phone, only to hear an unfamiliar voice on the other end say, "Excuse me, lady, I know I have the wrong number, but I just had to find out—who got the mouse?"

You probably had very little difficulty recognizing most of the irrelevant details in these practice stories because you were looking for them. We hope these exercises have helped raise your *awareness* of irrelevancy, so that you can recognize it when you hear it, even though you may not have been consciously listening for it.

As you become more aware of *distracting irrelevancies* when you hear them in the verbal communications of others, you will become more adept as a listener. As you become more aware of them in your own speech and more adept at eliminating them, you will make yourself an effective communicator.

• 16 •
Be Sensitive to the Needs of Others (Send a Care Package Today)

The wife of Benjamin Disraeli, the great English states-man, made a secret and very clever arrangement with one of her husband's associates. She asked him to notify her at the end of each day whenever Disraeli had a par-ticularly difficult session with the cabinet. She knew that on those days her husband would be coming home very tired and dispirited and in need of solace.

Whenever she received word that it had been one of those days, Mrs. Disraeli would go through the house and turn on every light in it, making the great house in which they lived sparkle. This thoughtful lady knew that the bright lights welcoming him home always lifted Disraeli's spirits and banished the problems of the day.

Now, that was a very understanding and caring wife. By putting her husband in a better mood by being so sensitive to *his* needs, she probably made him, in turn, more receptive to *her*. Too frequently what happens in the average household at the end of a hard day is more like a communications combat zone.

Luke lets himself into the house and calls out to his wife, "Chrissy, are you home?" As he hangs up his coat, he thinks, Boy, what a rotten day. We lost that contract after I worked on it for three months. My secretary is getting married next week and moving out of town. I'm not getting as much help as I need from that new tech writer I hired, and I'll probably have to prepare that important presentation myself. That means I'll have to work every night next week to get it done. I need to talk to Chrissy. I need to get this off my chest.

Chrissy is loudly slamming pots and pans around as she calls back to Luke, "I'm in the kitchen." She's thinking, Gosh, am I glad he's home. I got stuck in that expressway traffic on the way back from the orthodontist, and the car overheated because it needs a new radiator. I had to be towed to the repair shop. The orthodontist said the correction of Jimmy's overbite is going to cost three thousand dollars. The repairs for the car will be around four hundred dollars. We won't be able to take a vacation for at least two years! Besides, I dropped the meat loaf on the floor when I burned my hand taking the pan out of the oven. As soon as I clean up this mess, we'll have to go out for hamburgers. What I need is a little sympathy from Luke.

"Hi, Dad," Jimmy calls from his room, where he's been struggling hard to build a special project for the science fair at school. He's thinking, I'll bet Dad could tell me how to put this thing together so it will rotate the way it should. But before I ask him, I'm going to show Mom and Dad the perfect grade I got on the math test this morning. Boy, I sure studied hard for that. I've just been waiting until they were together so I could tell them.

"Chrissy, what's for supper?" Luke asks.

"You won't care about dinner after I tell you what happened to me today," Chrissy says.

"Mom, Dad, look! I got a perfect grade," Jimmy interrupts.

"That's real nice, son. Chrissy, I'm starved," Luke complains. "Doesn't a man have the right to expect dinner to be ready when he comes home from a hard day's work?"

"Mom . . ." Jimmy begins.

"I heard you, Jimmy. That's fine. Luke, I've had a perfectly awful day, and all you can think about is food," Chrissy accuses.

"Oh, for heaven's sake, all right, tell me about your perfectly awful day, if that's what it's going to take for me to get some dinner around here."

"Dad, I'm doing a project for the science fair and—"

"Later, Jimmy."

"We'll have to go out to eat," Chrissy says defensively.

"Okay, then, let's go. Jimmy, get your jacket and get in the car. Chrissy, are you going to tell me what happened?"

"Oh, just forget it," she says. "It isn't important."

By now Luke feels that his needs aren't important, either, and Jimmy is convinced that his needs aren't of any importance to either of his parents. Nobody here was listening to learn the needs of the others. What was taking place was an awful lot of tuning out, because no one was taking control and just *listening* to what was going on with the others. The messages were clear enough, but no matter how well someone is sending, if no one is receiving, there is no communication.

Now let's reconsider the scenario with one person in the role of the sensitive listener. Let's suppose that this time Chrissy is that person.

Luke lets himself into the house and calls out, "Chrissy, are you home?"

"I'm in the kitchen," she answers.

"Hi, Dad," Jimmy calls from his room.

"Chrissy, what's for supper?" Luke asks.

"You sound tired," Chrissy observes. "Did you have a rough day?"

"Mom, Dad, look! I got a perfect grade," Jimmy interrupts.

"That's real nice, son. Yeah, it was one of those days when nothing goes right. There was nothing but bad news."

"Me, too. And I dropped the meat loaf, so I don't

know what we're going to have for dinner. Why don't you fix us a nice cool drink, and then you can tell me about your day while I warm up something from the freezer." Chrissy turns to Jimmy. "Say, that's a good-looking paper. Isn't this the test you studied so hard for?"

"That's the one," Jimmy says, smiling.

"I'm so proud of you for that. I'll tell you what—why don't you set the table, and while you're doing that you can tell Dad and me about how school is going."

It would work just as well if Luke assumed the role of sensitive listener. If Luke was listening for the needs of others, it could go something like this:

"Chrissy, are you home?" Luke asks.

"I'm in the kitchen," she answers.

"Hi, Dad," Jimmy calls from his room.

"Chrissy, what's for supper?"

"You won't care after I tell you what happened to me today. I got stuck in traffic on the expressway on the way back from the orthodontist, and—"

"Mom, Dad, look! I got a perfect grade," Jimmy interrupts.

"That's real nice, son," Luke says, looking over the paper. "I know you studied very hard for this test, and I'm proud of you. Why don't you wash up, and then you can tell us about it while you set the table for dinner. Chrissy, you sound like your day wasn't any better than mine. Why don't I help you fix dinner while you tell me about it?"

As long as someone is in the role of sensitive listener, the communication will probably succeed. It doesn't matter who that person is, as long as *someone* is listening while the other one talks. In both examples where there was a listener, everyone was willing to wait for a turn to be heard. Each one could wait, knowing that a time would come to talk about his or her needs. When either of Jimmy's parents assumes the role of sensitive listener, they are teaching Jimmy, by example, an important communication skill.

Sometimes the person who needs to talk doesn't want

you to give him any feedback or take any action. He just wants a sympathetic ear in order to get something off his chest. He just wants to talk to somebody, and you don't have to say or do anything at all. When you find yourself in that sort of position, all you have to do is have *control*, saying to yourself, "I am just going to listen. I am not going to sit in judgment because although this might all seem very mundane to me, it is important to this person. I am going to let this person tell me all about it while I just *listen*."

Frequently this type of situation will come up in a business setting. Sometimes people in the other office just need to talk to someone, too, but don't need anyone either to sit in judgment or to give advice. In fact, don't give advice even if you're tempted. Giving advice can be dangerous. If you are caught in the middle, taking sides in someone else's dispute with a co-worker, friend, parent, child, lover or spouse, you can't win. There is no way you can get between the person and one of these other important people in his life and come out of it whole. If someone comes to you to talk about personal problems, don't take sides. If the people involved make up, they'll both be angry at you for involving yourself; if they split, they'll both be angry at you for involving yourself. Be discreet, be tactful and be quiet. Just *listen*. After they've worked out their problems, these people may even come back and thank you for being a good listener at a time when they needed one so very much.

There are some people who will take advantage of you for being a good listener. You may find these people darkening your office door much too frequently, coming in to talk too often and too long and taking up too much of your time. In these instances you will have to have control. You should not and must not allow people to take up your time constantly. That means you will have to use your judgment.

Louise, a word-processor operator, says through clenched teeth, "I hate my job! It's monotonous, it's routine, it's boring! My boss is a rat, and there's no room for advancement. I barely make enough money to pay my rent. Why I ever thought going to business school would get me anywhere, I'll never know. My mother was right when she told me to stay in Pitsville and marry my childhood sweetheart. He owns a hardware store now, and if I'd married him . . .''

Just listen. No comment necessary.

Of course, *sensitive listening* is really much more than just passive hearing. There are some noncommittal, sympathetic comments you can interject at the appropriate time that will validate the feelings of the other person, putting you with what the person is saying without putting you on either side of the issue:

"Yes, I see what you mean."
"That must have been exciting. Tell me more about it."
"I can understand why you would feel that way."
"That must be a difficult decision."

You can also ask questions that show you are interested and concerned but that will not get you personally involved.

"What happened then?"
"How did you feel?"
"What are your options?"
"What do you want to do?'

We repeat: you should not interrupt, or criticize, or argue, or ever offer advice. However, if you are asked for your opinion and it is important and appropriate to give it, give it very briefly and without taking sides, if at all possible. Then say no more. You can safely step out of the role of listener if you do it with care and sensitivity, but only when you're asked.

A final word on this kind of listening: having used your judgment to evaluate the other person's legitimate needs, and having decided that you are willing to be a sensitive listener for this person, let your listening be sincere. Let it be more that just letting your eyes stare blankly while you occasionally say, "Uh-huh, uh-huh." That's not really listening.

If the person is deserving of your time and attention, then give your time and attention in a generous spirit. We know what a busy person you are and that you've got problems of your own. But don't *you* sometimes need a sensitive listener to talk to, and aren't you glad when somebody is there? Somebody who really listens to you?

That's one of the most important elements of a friendship, one of the most important things a friend can do for you. It's great to have that kind of friend, and it's a great feeling to be that kind of friend.

The fringe benefit of listening to fulfill the needs of others is that when people are listened to with this kind of sensitivity, they tend to become more sensitive listeners themselves.

· 17 ·
Listen to Learn
the Interests of Others
(He's Brilliant! He Talks
About Me!)

There is a story about an insurance salesman who made a million-dollar sale to a doctor. He later said, in explaining to his co-workers how he had achieved this feat, "I followed the rule book. I did everything it recommends. Knowing what sticklers doctors can be, I made sure to arrive right on the button for our appointment. His waiting room was jammed with patients, but I wanted four hours just to get to see him, which he appreciated. He told me that it was a real pleasure for him to meet a salesman who knew how to conduct himself in a professional man's office. I smiled very warmly as I assured him that it was nothing at all, quite all right, and then I asked him about himself. I hung on his every word while he told me, and I bent over backward to agree with everything he said. He talked nonstop for three hours, and then he asked me if I would come back next week. I told him I wouldn't mind at all, that it would be no problem for me, and I left. I returned a week later and went through the same thing all over again. But when I left his office that time, I had not only made a sale, I had made a friend for life."

The salesman paused, then concluded, "But he'll never know what an enemy *he* made!"

Any number of ways have been proposed to us, by any number of experts, to make friends and influence people. Some of them, like the one used by the salesman in the story, involve an element of considerable self-sacrifice. If you do win someone over and make a favorable impression, and get what you want from him, you may find you have done so at high personal cost.

The salesman wasn't being completely honest with his business prospect, and the doctor wasn't really listening to the salesman. The result, even though the sale was made, was a horrible but accurate illustration of bad communications.

Good verbal communication is two-way. There can be no verbal communication without someone *listening*.

"Are you going to Barton's party tonight?" Betty asked.

"I certainly am," Lois answered enthusiastically. "Joe and I have been looking forward to meeting Barton's wife."

"Haven't you ever met Sandra?" Betty asked, surprised. "Well, I met her at a party a few months ago, and I can tell you that she is the biggest bore. She doesn't know anything except cleaning house, shopping for groceries and raising kids. My advice is don't get stuck trying to talk to her tonight."

That night Betty introduced Anne to Sandra. Betty noticed after a while that Anne and Sandra had been talking together for some time. Feeling duty-bound, Betty sent Joe over to them with instructions to "rescue Anne from that bore." Instead Joe joined their conversation. Then Betty sent Anne's husband, Rex, to the rescue, but he also stayed. Finally Betty approached the small group herself and asked Anne if she would mind helping her in the kitchen for just a moment.

Once they were in the kitchen, Betty confessed, "I really don't need your help, Anne. I was just trying to rescue you from Sandra. She's that bore I warned you about."

"Well, I thought that was the name you mentioned," Anne said. "But honestly, Betty, I couldn't believe she was the same person you were talking about. She's really interesting. She lived all over the world before she married Barton. She told us that her family was in the Philippines at the time the Japanese invaded. She studied art in France, and she still paints and even sold a piece recently. She has been to school in Switzerland and in England, too."

Betty had made the mistake of stereotyping Sandra on their first meeting. When she met her she *saw* a quiet, rather short, slightly plump, plainly dressed woman wearing a simple hairdo and very little makeup. She seemed to fit her expectations of women who stay at home and do nothing. Betty made no effort to find out if Sandra was anything but what she had assumed she was.

Anne, on the other hand, was a good listener to clues people give us about themselves. When Anne mentioned a painting she had bought recently, Sandra made a comment about the artist that was similar to what Anne had been told by the salesman at the gallery. Then Anne observed, "Sandra, you seem to know quite a bit about this artist's work. Where did you learn that?"

Sandra said that she had studied art in France some years ago, when her father was on a diplomatic assignment there. Anne heard another clue and asked about Sandra's father's career, and Sandra began to talk about other places she had been and things she had done.

When you walk into someone's office or home, you might see golf trophies on a shelf and decide that this person is interested in golf. If you see a mounted fish hanging on the wall, you would assume that the person is enthusiastic about fishing and use that to open a conversation. There are all kinds of visible clues people give us with their books, photographs, hobbies, even the jewelry they wear. You immediately have a visual clue and can start talking by commenting on it.

People also give us clues in conversation. They might

use a nautical term or a sports term; if you are listening for these verbal clues, you can pick up on them and have something to talk about.

You have to listen actively, for the interests of others can very easily go right by you. Three people can have a conversation, and the first person might walk away, like Betty, saying that there just wasn't anything to talk about. The second person, like Anne, will say, "But of course there was something to talk about. I can tell you a lot about him. Why, he is a journalism graduate, he's working in the copy room of the city newspaper, he's writing a novel based on his family's history, and . . ."

The third person had given at least three or four clues to his personality and interests, and yet one listener walked away feeling that she knew nothing about him, while the other picked up on every clue and an interesting conversation took place between them.

Some people catch the clues, and thus they have the advantage of being able to talk to anyone. Others don't, and they can only try to excuse themselves at the first opportunity, keeping the encounter as brief as possible. They will say that nothing good has happened between them and the other person, and they will be right.

You have to listen because you cannot know what people are like until they *tell* you. Getting to know people and learning to break the snap-judgment habit is like looking for buried treasure. It's there. Everyone, including you, is full of a variety of treasures in the form of interesting surprises, experiences, opinions and ideas.

Those experiences, opinions and ideas are the catalytic material that brings any two people together, whether it is yourself and another, or two others. Just as you can successfully employ those clues to open the communications between yourself and someone else, you can use them with equal effectiveness with two others.

We often have to make introductions. Beyond the basics of etiquette, where do you go after that? The answer is to go to those invaluable clues.

Perhaps you're at a business luncheon and talking to

a long-time associate when a new associate joins you and you have to introduce him. How do you do that and keep the conversation going, too? Perhaps you're the host or hostess at a party and you have to introduce the latest arrival to someone he doesn't know. How are you going to get the conversation started? Suppose you're at a conference or convention and you have to introduce two people, both of whom you work with but who don't know each other. What do they have in common?

You want to be able to say, after making the introduction at the business luncheon, "Ralph likes to play golf, too. I thought we might all get together for a game some weekend. What do you think, Lee?" (You had noticed Ralph's golf trophies in his office last week and had talked with him then about his interest in the game.)

At the party, you want to be able to say, "Ralph is thinking of buying a car just like yours, Mildred. What do you think of yours now after two years of driving it?" (You remembered that Ralph had asked you if you could recommend a dealership.)

At the conference or convention you want to be able to say, "Ralph has just transferred here from the Houston office. Didn't you troubleshoot there when they opened that branch, Marion?" You've made an introduction and helped keep the conversation going, using what you learned about Ralph when you met him and *listened for clues about him*.

There is probably no greater compliment that one person can pay another than the simple act of remembering something about him. And you will probably find that compliment being returned in several ways. As you become more skillful at listening for clues to others and using them, you will become a better communicator. Your career will benefit, your social life will expand and your list of admirers will grow. And if you're really lucky, they will all be listening for clues about you.

· 18 ·
Playing Through
(Make a Commitment)

All your life you have been listening unconsciously
because you thought that was the way the game was
played. Now you know better. You know there are
ground rules, the first of which is to start listening consciously, with organization.

Here is a list of all the concepts of organized listening
we have discussed in the previous chapters:

1. Learn the other person's name and use it.
2. Listen for filing purposes.
3. Listen to give information.
4. Don't be distracted by emotion-packed words.
5. Find and capitalize on points of agreement.
6. Listen for the hidden agenda.
7. Don't get taken in by false signals.
8. Listen for results.
9. Remember the power of silence.
10. Look for clues to the other person's mood.
11. Find the hotbutton.
12. Listen to yourself.
13. Don't be distracted by or use irrelevancies.

14. Be sensitive to fulfilling other people's needs.
15. Listen to find out the interests of others.

When you start on a regimen of exercise to improve your physical condition, you make it part of your daily routine. When you start on a reduced-calorie diet to lose weight, you make it part of your daily routine. But if you do not do the exercises or watch what you're eating every day, you will probably not improve your physical condition and you probably won't lose weight.

You now have the reigmen required for organizing your listening. Make it part of your daily routine, too. If you want to get the best results, use the fifteen concepts every day. Just as with exercise and dieting, the more consistently you practice, the more you will be able to take control and reap the benefits.

A routine is needed if you are to become an effective and consistent communicator. The one we suggest begins with you copying the list of listening concepts from the beginning of this chapter and keeping it in your desk drawer. Then on Monday morning take out the list and review your calendar for the upcoming week. Look for ways you can utilize the organized listening concepts. For example, if you see you are scheduled to attend a meeting on Tuesday and you know somebody will be bringing up some touchy points involving disputes and polarization of the group, write on your calendar: "Listen for points of agreement." Or if you know you're going to have to make a sales pitch at the meeting, write a reminder on the calendar: "No irrelevancies." On Wednesday afternoon an out-of-town representative is coming to town who always seems to put you on the defensive. Write: "Listen not to be distracted by emotion-packed words." Glancing at the calendar, you will be prepared when he comes in, and you will have control. On Friday you'll be going to a luncheon where there will be four or five people whom you have never met. Under the luncheon notation write: "Listen for names." Say to yourself, "I'm going to remember all the names of the people I'm going to meet at the luncheon.'' You will be programming yourself to succeed.

These concepts are frequently interrelated. They can't be separated into specific communications zones because they don't operate singly, and you're not going to get good results if you say, ''Today I'll just listen for the interests of others, and tomorrow I'll pay attention to moods.'' They have to be coordinated. For example, while you are looking for points of agreement at the Tuesday meeting, someone who is nodding his head and saying, ''I see what you mean'' or ''That's a good point'' can unintentionally be giving you false signals.

By looking at each of these concepts every week and writing down the ones you are going to use, you will increase your awareness, bringing them to a level of consciousness where they are more available to you. Then you can choose and use many different combinations. It's like mastering a new sport: a book can tell you how to volley in tennis, but to play a good game you must be consciously aware of many techniques and then practice until some things become automatic. That's our point here: in communication, as in a sport, you need to know and understand the concepts, practice them constantly and then achieve consistent control.

So *think through* your entire week and program yourself to use these concepts of organized listening whenever and wherever you can. If you do this consistently week after week, soon it will become automatic. It's good self-management, and that's where good management really begins: with yourself.

· 19 ·

First Impressions, Last Words (No Time to Be All Thumbs with Your Mouth)

As a rule, you make up your mind about a new acquaintance and draw your initial impression in the first one to three minutes with him. Unconsciously, we appraise the other person and know that we're being appraised in turn in those first few minutes. It's a lot like auditioning for a part without having read the script.

A virtual mountain of first impressions forms in our minds which we might have no second chance to change, reverse or reconstruct. The first impression in many instances is the last word. In every face-to-face encounter between two or more people, we have about three minutes to move a mountain of rapidly forming impressions and opinions into an affirmative position on the other person's mental map of who we really are. Lawyers say that cases are won or lost in the first three minutes of their first words spoken to a jury.

Granted, that's a very short audition. But, realistically, that's about the size of it. We've got three minutes to sell ourselves in any given situation in life: business, professional, social or personal. This is no time to be all thumbs with your mouth.

It doesn't take much calculating to see that what we say in those first three minutes is going to have a great deal to do with the sale: whether we succeed in selling a generally pleasant, positive impression about ourselves or come up sounding like a candidate for remedial education. No wonder talking to each other scares so many of us. We seldom hear ourselves until it's too late.

Added to the immediacy of first impressions is the conservative estimate that at least fifty percent of what we say every day is misunderstood or misinterpreted by the people we say it to. Take the fellow who walked into a department store and asked the first salesperson he met, "Excuse me, could you tell me where the rest rooms are?" Misunderstanding him, she thought he had asked for the restaurants and replied, "There's one on the top floor if you want to sit down, and one on the ground floor, under the stairs, if you want to stand up."

If we're only accurately understood about half the time—about ninety seconds of those estimated first three minutes we have in which to sell ourselves—then it's easy to see that frequently we can't even be sure which were the ninety seconds that counted.

We all tend to make judgments about other people in a flash, the way a camera gives its subject a single frame in which to justify itself. Take the case of the old man, dressed in overalls and weatherbeaten straw hat, who strolled into the small town's newly opened bank, announcing that he wanted to talk to somebody.

"Yes, of course, Mr. Smith, let me introduce you to our Mr. Baker," said the receptionist with a smile, settling the old farmer in a chair next to the young vice-president's desk.

Mr. Baker, who was new in town, passed a few minutes in easy conversation about the weather and the condition of crops as he worked his way into a series of questions. After inquiring as to whether Mr. Smith owned his farm and how much land the farm included, he continued, "And do you own a car, Mr. Smith?"

"Yep, a 1932 model."

"Is that the only vehicle you own?" Baker pursued as he wrote the information out on a form.

"No, I've got a 1940 model pickup sitting out under the shed, but I don't use it much anymore," Smith replied calmly.

"Well, Mr. Smith, don't you have any other collateral? I don't think we can make a loan based on what I've written down here."

"Loan, hell! I came in here to put money *in* this bank, not take it out!" roared the old man.

Hearing the commotion, the bank president quietly but quickly took the young vice-president aside, explaining that Mr. Smith had an oil well that stood right next to the shed and the 1940 model pickup. Further, he said that Mr. Smith owned several other oil wells on several other pieces of property, and that Mr. Smith undoubtedly could buy and sell the bank and everybody in it any day of the week, and would Mr. Baker please refrain from making snap judgments about the bank's customers in the future.

A rule in the first-impression game is not to make snap judgments before you make conversation. Try to avoid casting the other person in a role based on your first impression. Such split-second casting calls are usually based on appearances, and we all know what happens when you judge a book by its cover: you miss a lot of great stories.

Our first impressions of others, and theirs of us, are based almost entirely on two things: what we say and how we appear. Our appearance—how we look and sound to other people—is a composite of the clothes we wear, any noticeable accent in our voice and our general attitude—whether we seem to be shy, outgoing, overbearing, egotistical, withdrawn or whatever. We depend a great deal on appearances in drawing first impressions because at first encounter we don't have anything else to go on.

But appearances can be deceiving. A woman we met at a convention told the story of running into an old high-school chum in a grocery store some twenty years later. "Of course, there she was, perfectly groomed and wearing something casually chic in a shade of green that set off her dark auburn hair to perfection. I, on the other hand, having run to the store in a state of minor emergency, looked as if I'd just stepped out of a hurricane, wearing a shade of disarray that set off the circles under my eyes to perfection. In my dismay at being caught in such a condition, I felt I was stammering and stuttering and had developed all the personality of a stop sign. My initial impression was that *she* had probably looked this smashing every single day of her life during the twenty years since graduation. And my second impression was that she was probably thinking the same about me!" Over the years the woman who told us this story had actually become quite successful in her career, but that was smothered by the first impression.

At one time or another we've all heard someone say, "I can read people like an open book," or "I'm a great judge of character. I can tell a lot about people at a glance." That's putting a lot of faith in your powers of observation. If you think you're a pretty good natural observer, check yourself out on these items:

1. All of us at one time or another have had our temperature taken. What are the lowest and highest numbers on the usual oral thermometer?
2. Whose face appears on a $10 bill?
3. On most dial telephones there are letters with numbers. What letters are above the number 3?
4. If you turn the dial on your AM radio, what are the lowest and highest numbers?
5. There are fifty stars on the American flag, arranged in rows. How many stars are in each row?

The answers are at the end of this chapter. If you

answered all the questions correctly, give yourself a high rating for observation ability.

Regardless of your observation ability, however, you're likely to be wrong more often than right where first impressions of people are concerned, so remember to make conversation, not snap judgments.

For the interested person who makes himself more than just an observer, getting to know someone is like looking for buried treasure. He knows there's more there than meets the eye, so he doesn't rely on appearances alone but tries to look deeper, to discover the shared common interests or the fascinating diversities of the stranger he's met.

How? Following is an exercise that stretches your powers of observation and your imagination, usually with very surprising results.

1. On a piece of paper write down the names of the three or four people you've met most recently, in any business or social setting; preferably people you're likely to meet again.
2. Under each name write down your first impression of that person in each of these three categories: (a) probable taste in music; (b) probable hobby; and (c) probable favorite drink.

Leave no room to put down later corrections of these first impressions, because very few people turn out to be much as we imagine them to be at first glance. The man you've got pegged as a sure-fire beer drinker may turn out to be a wine connoisseur, and the woman you thought probably drank tea all day may like her Scotch straight up. So much for appearances.

Consider yourself. How do you think someone else would answer those three questions based on a first impression of you? In fact, you could reverse the procedure and ask one or two of your newer acquaintances to join in your experiment by giving you their first impressions of your probable tastes and hobbies. Finding out how close to the mark you are about each other might well lead to the most interesting conversation you've had in a long time. It could also lead to a new friendship.

Meeting new people, individually or in groups, doesn't have to be a three-minute casting call where everyone just shows up and waits to be judged by the other fellow on whether or not he merits a longer audition. Meeting new people can be your opportunity to offer an impression of yourself as a person who's interested in others—a treasure hunter.

First impressions don't have to be last words. You can help control the situation by remembering and repeating the other person's name. This immediately shows that you find the person valuable. You also gain control by refusing to make snap judgments or superficial assumptions based on appearances and by being interested enough to look for the buried treasure in each personality you meet, drawing other people out. By doing these simple things, can't you already see what an interesting and confident person you are in their eyes? That's the last word on first impressions.

Answers to Questions on Page 146:

1. 94 to 108
2. Alexander Hamilton
3. DEF
4. 54 to 160
5. Five rows of six stars alternating with four rows of five stars

· 20 ·
The Art of Conversation
(For Openers)

The art of talking to people consists of spontaneity built on preparation. It's no accident that some people are great conversationalists. They're prepared to be. Although their opening remark always seems to be spontaneous, if the truth were known, they are probably using their own personal formulas of conversational cue cards. This is the same sort of mental inventory we discussed regarding listening for filing purposes—a store of verbal gambits kept in the file cabinet of the mind.

That's not to say that it's a stock inventory that never changes. On the contrary, it's the kind of reference material that grows and changes all the time. Once you develop the habit, you keep adding mental files to your inventory from almost everything you read or hear. You can make conversation in all kinds of weather without talking *about* the weather, through developing the habit of preparation. And it can be as much fun as taking up any other new hobby.

How you go about preparing your own conversational file is a matter of personal choice. How long it will take you is a matter of point of view.

Appearances, as we know, can be deceiving. So can conversation, in one respect. By using one small conversational cue card as an opener, you can appear to be a conversational whiz when all you really have done is gotten the ball rolling.

The sources from which you develop conversational cue cards are almost limitless. Here are just a few, for openers:

One of the best places to start is with other people's interests. Consider the circumstances that have brought you together. Have you met at a business or civic luncheon? At the office? A committee meeting? A friend's home? What common denominators of interest might you share with this new acquaintance?

There are two very good reasons for beginning your search for a topic of conversation with other people's interests: first, it offers them a first impression of you as a person who values other people, a person who always finds other people interesting; second, by indicating your interest in them, you automatically put them at ease. You've skillfully removed that awkward moment when they are concerned about what kind of impression they're making and what kind of judgment you're drawing from that impression. You've taken the lead, and they're probably relieved and delighted.

A source of conversation when there are no immediately apparent common denominators of interest might be fascinating differences. Does the person have an interesting accent? Has he just ordered iced coffee at the luncheon, while everyone else opted for iced tea? "Where did you develop a taste for iced coffee?" you ask. "In this part of the country no one but my mother has drunk iced coffee as long as I can remember." He laughs as he replies, "Well, I haven't been in this part of the country long enough to know the rules yet. Our company just relocated its main office here last month. We're still getting settled." You're already into a conversation before you've had the time to worry about how to get started.

Of course, if you're meeting someone on his own

ground, in his office or home, you have the opportunity to draw on observation as a source of conversation. You've been waiting in the reception area for a few minutes, let's say, and have just been ushered into the office of the man you came to meet. You've already shaken hands (and found a pleasant way to repeat his name) when you say, "That's a beautiful trophy fish you have mounted in the entrance area. A sailfish, isn't it? Your catch?"

"Yes, he is a beauty, isn't he? Caught him in the Gulf last year," your prospective customer says. "Are you a fisherman, too?"

"No, to tell you the truth, Mr. Miller, I'm scared to death of deep water. Probably comes from being a poor swimmer," you say. "Have you always been a fisherman, or did you recently take it up?"

"Why, I've been fishin' since God invented the fishin' pole. I grew up with the smell of saltwater; thought it was perfume till I was fifteen."

You already know what your man's hobby is, and if you're paying attention you will have noticed that he's a bit poetic about it. Fishing is his love, not just his hobby. You're off and running. Of course, this opener could just as easily have been an observation on a piece of art, an embroidered wall motto or the photo on that corner table of the young girl on the white horse.

One of the easiest ways to open a conversation is to offer the other person a compliment. This serves to show your immediate interest in him as well as your thoughtful observation. There is one definitive rule to this strategy: be sincere. But it's easy to play the game by that rule. You can always find something sincerely complimentary to say to another person if you make the effort, and it can be very rewarding in a number of ways: it will probably make you feel as good as the person you complimented, and you will immediately put the other person at ease. Some people are most comfortable when they don't realize they're having a conversation, when an exchange of remarks just flows naturally and becomes a conversation. The skillful conversationalist is one who can lead with an opening remark that seems spontaneous and easy, allowing the other person a comfortable response. A compliment, which is really just another cue based on an observation, is often the answer in an awkward situation with a shy person. About half of real communication skill involves putting the other person at ease, being enough in control of your thoughts to make the first move. For openers, you can't go wrong with thoughtfulness.

Aside from being interested and observant where other people are concerned, you can use other sources and techniques to help you prepare conversational cue cards. The tools of any craft are usually assumed to be complex and intricate and usually are not. So it is with conversation. The person who considers himself a novice in the art of conversation usually assumes that the accomplished craftsman—the true conversationalist—has some special knowledge, some secret, that separates him from the conversational strugglers. If he does—and it is possible to look at it that way—his special tool is reading.

The English essayist Joseph Addison (1672–1719) said, "Reading is to the mind what exercise is to the body." The American author F. B. Sanborn (1831–1917) expanded on that thought when he said, "The careful reader of a few good newspapers can learn more in a year than most scholars do in their great libraries."

While we would not argue about the amount or the depth of knowledge that a true scholar attains, we would point out that the scholar is usually pursuing a specific field of interest, a single track of reading. The good conversationalist, on the other hand, is more of a dilettante, a person who dabbles in a subject, or many subjects, for his own enjoyment. The dilettante, as a reader, delves into a lot of subjects, seeking a wide variety of information and knowledge. He won't become an expert on anything, but he will be an interesting talker. For instance, you don't have to join the diplomatic corps to be conversant on foreign policy—just read the newspapers with some regularity. You don't have to be a stockbroker or a financier to know what the current interest rates are—just skim the business pages. You don't have to read every new book that comes out to be conversant on new books and authors—just read the weekly book review pages of a couple of major metropolitan newspapers.

Variety is the spice of life where conversation is concerned. A variety of selected reading enables you to talk about major events in the world, which affect other people in other places, as well as relating those events to the daily lives of yourself and your friends. Think of all the conversational cue cards that could be developed by just skimming the daily paper.

If you're thinking to yourself, Yeah, that's great for openers, but what do I follow it with? remember that conversation is designed to be a give-and-take affair. Good conversation doesn't require you to know enough about a subject to give a dissertation on it at the drop of a hat. In fact, the person who goes on and on at length on a subject often seems to be monopolizing the conversation. The person who hits on a topic of conversation that he knows a great deal about, turning the give-and-take into all give, may not realize that he's monopolizing the game, but his listeners will grow restive.

Being a dilettante reader is part of developing conversational cue cards; it is also one of the best ways to be prepared to make an interesting, spontaneous remark that can open a stimulating conversation. The dilettante reads and stores up other items besides current events and news. Among them may be epigrams, bits of trivia and humorous anecdotes. However, there are times when you certainly don't want to open with a lightweight or an inconsequential remark. There are certain times, and perhaps certain gatherings, when nothing fits the occasion quite so well as an informed remark. Let's say your neighbor is a psychologist, and he and his wife have invited you to a holiday cocktail party at their home, which will probably be populated by a good many of their friends in his profession. How in the world are you going to handle that conversational challenge?

A specialized challenge, when the subject doesn't happen to be your specialty, has a two-part answer. First, some brief directed reading on your part the evening before the party will undoubtedly provide you with a few stimulating questions to ask. In this instance you might pick up a recent copy of *Psychology Today* at a newsstand. In fact, there are specialty magazines being published today on almost everything under the sun, if you really want to bone up on what a specialized group may be discussing.

The second part of the answer to this kind of "specialized" problem is to remember that if the subject is not your specialty, you've been invited as a person, not as a member of a peer group. You're not expected to be a whiz kid on psychology. Therefore the most complimentary behavior is to show your interest in the guests, draw them out, give *them* a chance to talk. Read just enough before the party to ask one or two interesting questions, and let them take it from there. Be an interested listener. Above all, remember that each person is an individual, no matter what kind of specialty may have brought the group together. They are people very much like you, with common interests in kids, or house plants, or yard problems, or business management problems. With just enough directed reading to allow you to show an interest in their field or specialty, you can move on to conversation about your common interests, your fascinating differences, observations, graceful compliments—a whole host of conversational cue cards.

A friend of ours suggests that if you read one good daily newspaper, one or two syndicated columnists, one news magazine a month and a regional or city magazine centered on your area of the country, you can talk to anyone about anything, anytime, anywhere. We would also advise you to watch a talk show every now and then and be prepared to do some occasional directed reading. Remember, the art of talking to people is spontaneity built on preparation.

A word about organization: relax. Even if you're well read, well ahead, you will occasionally find yourself trying to remember a clever remark when suddenly your mind turns to scrambled eggs and you're having trouble remembering how many fingers are on your left hand. Or you may be trying to quote a statistic, a source, an author or a name when you suddenly feel as if someone just erased your brain. Relax. It happens to everyone at one time or another, even the best conversationalists. Keep in mind that making conversation with people is not going to be followed by a test. When you can't remember specifically, just say so. Don't hold up the flow of the conversation while you—and finally the other person too—agonize over trying to remember. When you feel as if you've gotten yourself into a trap, look how easy it is to get out of it:

"I read a timely comment in the paper the other day about that [whatever you've been discussing]. I can't remember whose column it was in, but he said [you paraphrase the remark]." You see, you really don't have to be that specific to get the remark or the thought into the conversation.

"We were playing this incredible trivia game at my sister-in-law's house the other night, and someone brought up the old saw about how deep is the ocean, how high is the sky? I can't remember the exact figures, but did you know the ocean is actually something over six miles deep? And the layer of air we breathe is about ten miles high, not counting several hundred miles of atmosphere above that? I was really amazed."

"Something over" is a good way to round off a specific figure when you can't remember it all, and "several hundred miles" makes your point without you spending the whole evening becoming a bore just trying to remember that it is actually more than six hundred miles of atmosphere. The point is, be as accurate as you can be and as honest as possible. Don't be a boring perfec-

tionist. The main point of your remark is that you were
amazed and surprised by the actual depth of the ocean
and the height of the sky. Say so and move on, or give
the other person time to respond. You don't have to be
trapped by details.

You made it to your neighbor's holiday party and
mistaking you for a psychiatrist, a man walks up to you
and says, "What do you think about Erich Fromm's
idea on psychic symbiotic union?"

"I have absolutely no idea what you're talking
about," you might say, "but it sounds fascinating. Tell
me about it."

When someone else opens a conversation and you
really don't have any idea or reference to the subject at
all, never try to fake it. You'll only dig a deep conversational hole. You're bound to bury yourself. Always be
open and candid. If you don't know, don't have an
opinion, or never even heard of the subject, just say so.
It's that easy. Being candid also offers you the opportunity to draw the person out, letting him talk about
something that obviously interests him. Being interested
in what someone else has to say is always complimentary, and you can't go wrong with a compliment. The
conversational opener is a sport all to itself, but the ball
doesn't always have to be in your court.

· 21 ·

Verbal Essence
(Tongue in Cheek)

Giving and Receiving Feedback

The organist was giving a concert, and he was playing brilliantly. During the intermission he looked at the man whose job it was to pump the organ as he played. The pumper said to the musician, "We're giving quite a performance, aren't we?"

"What do you mean *we*," the musician replied. "*I'm* the one who is giving the concert!"

After the intermission he returned to the stage, raised his hands dramatically and then brought them down on the keys. But there was no sound. Looking behind the organ, he saw the other man just sitting there, doing nothing.

"You're right," the organist admitted. "*We* are giving the concert."

Getting and giving feedback during communication is similar to the relationship between the man who plays the organ and the man who pumps it. Nothing can be accomplished if they don't work together.

Feedback is extremely important in communication

157

because it is the only way we have of determining whether we are hearing each other and what we are hearing each other say. Without feedback, either positive or negative, there can be no communication. Feedback provides the clues that tell us whether the listener is with us or whether he is completely lost regarding what we are trying to say. Feedback tells us whether we are understanding each other, whether we are in agreement or disagreement, whether we are getting the information we want or need, whether we're on the right track and whether we're going too fast or too slow.

Feedback is essential to keep communication going. Sometimes the feedback is as simple as a sound such as *hmmm* or a single word like *yes* or *oh*. Have you ever noticed that when you are listening to someone speak on the telephone, someone who has a great deal to say that you must listen to, you will interject those little words or sounds? You've probably also noticed that if you don't, the other person will stop to ask, "Are you there?"

Effective communication has been defined as "that which exists between two people when the message being sent is *received and interpreted the way it was intended.*" But how can we test the accuracy if we don't give and get feedback? So many things can go wrong. We don't always say things exactly as we mean them, and our intentions are not always clear to the listener. Each person knows what he meant to say, but he must draw inferences about what the other person meant to say.

Take the case of the woman who went to her lawyer to sue her husband for divorce. The lawyer asked, "Do you have grounds?"

The woman said, "I own two acres off Walnut Hill."

The lawyer asked, "Do you have a grudge?"

The woman said, "I have a carport that holds two cars."

The lawyer asked, "Does your husband beat you up?"

The woman said, "I'm up a half-hour before he is every morning."

The lawyer asked, "Why do you want a divorce?"

The woman said, "I can't communicate with him."

There are some techniques that help in getting and giving feedback. We can repeat and rephrase what we heard the other person say, being sure that we have given him time to finish first. Cutting in too soon may cut off some information that is important for understanding. By rephrasing you are simply expressing your understanding, in your own words, without judgment or interpretation. After understanding has been verified, then we can go on to the next level of the communication.

An accountant told a colleague that he was very disappointed with the caliber of men and women who were coming out of business school.

"I bring them into my office, tell them the facts and the problem I want to research and ask them if they understand. They always say yes, but when they return they have researched the wrong question." It finally occurred to this accountant that maybe he wasn't getting enough feedback. He thought about what was happening in his communications with his employees. He was aware that he could appear stern and unapproachable, and he realized that he was in the habit of asking bluntly, *"Do you understand?"* His listeners, of course, were afraid to admit that they didn't, with the result that they frequently mishandled matters. So he started making them more comfortable by saying, "I'm not sure that I have made this clear. What is your understanding of what I'm looking for?" This technique took his listener off the defensive so that the person could feel comfortable about asking questions when he didn't understand. Now the accountant has learned to give and receive feedback, and he *verifies* what he and his young associates say to each other.

Thinking Things Through

He was considered a front runner for his party's nomination as presidential candidate. His pro-Vietnam War stance and his political position as the governor of a large state gave him the right profile, and his campaign was going well. He was definitely a man to be reckoned with. The media followed him everywhere, recording every move he made and every word he spoke.

One day he announced that he'd had a change of attitude, and he was now in opposition to United States involvement in the Vietnam conflict.

A reporter asked, "Governor, why did you think the war was all right in the first place?"

"I was brainwashed," was the reply. The press picked up on that one word and capitalized on the public's negative view of it. From that point on the governor was no longer a challenge to the other presidential aspirants.

We all make mistakes, of course, even when we're trying to be very careful. It's also true that the higher our aspirations and the more we are attempting to achieve, the more we have at risk and the more we stand to lose. But very often just a little more thinking through of all the possible consequences might prevent some of those disastrous errors.

Psychologists have demonstrated under controlled experimental conditions that mentally picturing ahead actually does improve performance and gives people more control over what they do. In one study people were seated before a dartboard and told to aim darts mentally at it. Later, when they threw real darts at the target, it was found that their aim had improved as much as it would have had they actually been throwing the darts all the time.

Another illustration of this is found in what we see golfers do before they actually stroke the ball. We can see the golfer rehearsing his move, imagining what will happen—mentally picturing what he will do and what the outcome will be. And then, more often than not, the golfer is able to do exactly the right thing to put the ball precisely where he wants it to go.

The difference between success and failure can often be determined in those brief moments when, like the golfer, we think ahead about where we want to aim our communications and what effect we want them to have.

It may take only a few moments to do that, but each moment truly can be worth an hour. Not only are communication skills tremendously improved, but we can also gain increased control over our decision-making abilities, especially in unexpected or critical situations. Decisions, as well as communications, can be increasingly on target.

One successful executive told us that he attributes his ability to say the right thing to his habit of taking ten seconds to think before he speaks. Only ten seconds! What a small cost in terms of time and self-discipline in order to have that kind of control over his communications.

Even in the midst of the sometimes frenetic activity of the high-pressure world of business, it is possible to take those few important moments. Rarely is any emergency of such a life-and-death nature that we can't pause ten seconds to think before speaking or acting. And the habit of taking time to think things through can even have a calming effect that actually will facilitate communication.

By thinking through, you can save yourself from making a false start. If you walk into someone's office and just start talking to that person without having first thought about what you are going to say, you may have to stop and do some backtracking. The trouble is that even though you start all over again, the other person will very likely still be thinking about what you said earlier.

Take the time to think through what you want to say before you say it. Say it exactly the way you want to, and take one more step toward keeping control over your communications.

Giving an Overview

"We'll have to take six design engineers and put them on the third shift immediately," Lucas blurted out after rushing into his boss's office. "And we'll have to suspend all other computer use for at least a month. There will be problems, but the only alternative is to go outside to a computer consultant firm, and their best estimate is—''

''Wait a minute,'' the program manager said. ''I don't have the slightest idea what you are talking about.''

When someone rushes into someone else's office as Lucas did and starts right in talking a mile a minute, the other person can only feel overwhelmed by details about a situation he probably knows nothing about.

Suppose Lucas had walked into his boss's office and prepared him for the details by giving him an *overview* of the problem first.

''Five months ago when the cooling system failed and the computer went down, we lost six weeks' worth of work. We have recouped two weeks, but we're still one month behind. If we don't recoup the rest quickly, we're going to miss the major milestone for this quarter and put a million-dollar billing in jeopardy.''

Now the program manager knows what Lucas has come to talk about. ''I see,'' he says. ''What idea do you have?''

''We could go to a computer consultant firm, but their best estimate is $280,000. What I suggest is that we take six design engineers and put them on the third shift. We should then suspend all other computer uses for a month until we get this done.''

''All right, then,'' the program manager says. ''Let's do it.''

If you really want to sell what you have come to say, then your immediate need is to get the other person's attention, not to confuse him with a deluge of details which appear to be unrelated to a specific point. Since the overview is the germ of what you want to say, it can usually be accomplished rather quickly and with a minimum of words. In fact, the fewer the words, the better.

It shouldn't take a lot of words to give a good overview. One of the most effective campaign speeches ever made—and probably also the briefest—was entirely an overview. Thomas Buckley, running for the office of auditor in Massachusetts in 1941, said simply, "I am an auditor, not an orator." Buckley was elected and re-elected many times.

Before you walk into somebody's office, think about what you are going to talk about and prepare an overview. That is, prepare to tell him what the whole picture looks like. After he knows what it is that you have come to talk about, after you have his attention and his thinking is on the same wave length as yours, then go into the details.

Just the Facts

"Fred, can we get together tomorrow for lunch to talk about an idea I have for your advertising campaign?" John asked.

"All right," Fred answered. "But I'll be out of the office all morning. Where can we meet?"

"How about at the front door to the First National Bank at noon?"

"Fine. See you then."

At noon the next day Fred was waiting at the front door for John. And at twelve fifteen. And at twelve thirty. This is strange, he thought. John is usually so punctual.

Around the corner, John was looking at his watch and wondering what was keeping Fred.

Each of the men was waiting at what was, according to his own perception, the front door to the First National Bank. Who was right and who was wrong? Neither. They just weren't *specific* when they were making their plans to meet for lunch.

Being specific is somewhat similar to designing and constructing a building. The architect must know exactly what kind of house he is building before he can plan its structural lines. For example, if he is going to build a split-level house, then the foundation, floor plan, walls and roof will differ structurally from an English Tudor home. So the architect has to have all the specifics before designing the house on paper. Once he has laid out the floor plan, he can't go back and add another room or move a closet without having to do the whole plan over. Remember that whenever a change has to be made, it is done at considerable expense and loss of time.

In business communications, being specific is very much like informing the architect. It means that we are putting the other person in possession of all the facts that are relevant. It means that everything of importance is included—all pertinent information—so that there are no surprises. If we leave out any details, we then have to bring them up after a decision has been made or a plan has been outlined, saying "Oh, I almost forgot to mention . . ." When we do that, we are giving others an unpleasant shock that can be costly to the company.

Being specific is a way of being well organized that enables people to cover more ground and give more needed information in less time. And whenever you can get your message across clearly and concisely, other people will appreciate not only your courtesy and consideration but also your remarkable efficiency. And that has never done harm to anyone's career.

Find the Common Ground

When Franklin Delano Roosevelt was having trouble with a senator who was blocking some legislation, he learned that they had a common interest in stamp collecting. One night FDR got out his own collection and telephoned the senator to ask for his help. The senator was pleased to have been asked, and he and FDR spent the evening together working on the stamp collection. When the roll-call vote on that bill was taken the next day, the senator voted for it, although at no time during the evening had either man mentioned the bill. They had simply spent the evening sharing common ground and had become friends.

We can see the same sort of thing at any social gathering, because people do relate to each other on common ground. Two lawyers will find each other and retry their cases. Two doctors will find each other and make diagnoses.

But a writer and a sociologist can also find common ground in a discussion of the causes of poverty and unemployment, and a minister and an actor can discuss the morality of a new film. A teacher and a housewife can talk about their vacations, one on the beach at Waikiki and the other at the beach at Puerto Vallarta.

Remember the ease with which you made friends when you were a child? You were using common ground. Remember the ease with which you got to know those people from your hometown when you accidentally found each other in Europe on vacation? That was common ground.

Common ground can be cultural or educational. It can be a language. It can be a shared viewpoint. It can be many things, but, whatever it is, it is always grounds for communication.

Communication is facilitated by the common ground of language. For example, one person may be in sales and the other in production, but when they find that they both have a background in teaching, they gain a terminology they can use together. But words have different meanings for different people, and viewpoints affect the meaning of words. An awareness of these differences when you are looking for a common-ground language is important. For example, what is called congestion in a subway is called intimacy in a nightclub.

An American visitor to England was driving through London with his English friend, and the friend observed that the windscreen needed cleaning.

"You mean the windshield," the American corrected.

"Well, over here we call it a windscreen," the Englishman said.

"Then you are wrong," the American said, "because

we Americans invented the automobile and we call it a windshield."

"That's quite true," the Englishman countered, "but just remember who invented the *language.*"

Another example is the story of three men, each of whom saw the Grand Canyon from the viewpoint of their different occupations.

The archaeologist looked at it and said, "What a wonder of science."

The clergyman said, "One of the glories of God."

The cowboy saw it as "a heck of a place to lose a cow."

Psychologists tell us that one of the most important characteristics of well-adjusted people is their ability to reach out and relate to others. Corporations place high value on people who have that ability. They know that the person who cannot relate to others can't get along with others or work well with them, either.

The ability to see things through the other person's eyes, to understand his viewpoint as if it were your own, is a stepping-stone to success. Your career could pivot on the axis of your ability to find common ground with other people.

Have Patience

Marcus Aurelius (121–180), a wise Roman, wrote, "I am going to be meeting people today who talk too much —people who are selfish, egotistical, ungrateful. But I won't be surprised or disturbed, for I can't imagine a world without such people."

In business, people frequently will be involved in working on something very important and will be disturbed by a series of interruptions, and it often seems that as the deadline draws closer, people intrude more and more and the tension builds. Then comes irritation and, finally, exasperation.

We've all experienced that sort of thing. No one has

an infinite supply of patience, so it wouldn't be normal never to feel impatient. But there are ways of controlling it, and that's a goal worth seeking. Uncontrolled impatience can be very destructive, to us and to others.

A young man in his twenties found a job he'd always wanted. It was as assistant personnel director in the XYZ Corporation. The salary was generous, and there were opportunities for advancement. His educational background indicated that he should be able to develop in the position and perform well.

The personnel director hired him with some reservations about his experience, and, unfortunately, the personnel director was not a patient person. He kept an eye on the young man every minute. Every time the new employee made a mistake, the director was there to witness it and to criticize. As the young man became more and more nervous, he began to make more and more mistakes. Finally the director called him into his office and fired him because he was "just not doing the job as well as expected."

The young man was fortunate enough to find another job in a similar field. This time he had a more patient manager, and he quickly rose through the ranks. Twenty years later the XYZ Corporation asked him to join them as their new executive vice-president.

We're all fallible, because we're all human beings. But we can know that and be more patient with ourselves and with each other. If we try to stretch ourselves or each other beyond our limits, we break like a stretched rubber band.

Many times we become impatient about things over which we and others have no control, like waiting for the phone to ring, watching a pot boil or waiting for someone else to do something. And too many times people think only of their own needs when they are under pressure to perform, and then the world seems to be a dog-eat-dog place. The person who can go out of his way to take control of that pressure, to be considerate of other people's feelings, is helping himself in two ways: he is being a better person, and he will actually get what he needs sooner than if he resorted to pushing and nagging and making everyone nervous.

Have you ever played bridge and sat across from a partner who was impatient with you? When you were trying to bid, your partner started saying, "Come on, hurry up. We don't have all day." The more impatient your partner became, the more you worried about what he thought and said. Then your playing became even more erratic. You made mistakes that you had never made before because you couldn't concentrate on the game. Of course, this only resulted in your partner becoming more annoyed with you.

In business sometimes someone will stand over another person, saying, "Come on. Hurry up. We haven't got all day." The person under such pressure becomes less and less efficient because he is nervous and distracted. When he stops to try to ask a question like, "I'm not quite sure of this. How—" the other person cuts him off impatiently with, "I have already told you how." That may be true, but how is he going to get the job done without the information?

Patience is not necessarily the same as being long-suffering. You needn't let yourself be walked on or generally mistreated; be assertive when appropriate, yet patient when it will do the most good.

Impatience can destroy trust, and without trust, there is little or no communication. Without trust, people are wary of giving information and suspicious when receiving it. Communication promotes trust because it is itself based on trust. You promote that trust and improve communication by being patient.

Putting It Simply

A newspaper editor received a telegram that said, "Big story here on natural disaster. Shall I send?" The editor wired back, "Send 600 words."

The young reporter in the field sent another message: "Can't be told in less than 1200 words."

The editor's second message settled the disagreement: "Story of creation of world told in 600. Try it."

That advice applies just as well to business communications. The best words are the ones that everyone understands, and the best sentences are the ones that are short enough for everyone to comprehend.

Why *everyone?* Because in business there are people not only in our own but in other departments, for whom we work or who work for us, with whom we have to interrelate. We have to talk to people, *communicate* with people, all up and down the corporate ladder.

And outside business we have to talk to people in the community who may not understand what we are talking about. But it is often essential that they understand, and it may be our responsibility to explain it to them so that they can. That means we have to be able to *simplify.*

With the rapid escalation of technology these days, there is a constant input of terminology, numbers, letters, code words, abbreviations, acronyms, shortcuts and jargon that are peculiar to our specific businesses. Many professional people become accustomed to writing and thinking in that technical jargon and develop a tendency to use words only others in the same profession are likely to understand. While jargon is helpful to those within the profession, it is usually totally confusing to people outside it.

When an artist talks to an architect about "nativist impulse" or "national self-definition," and the architect talks to the artist about "an interpretive tool of a creative act with constraints of doctrinaire modernism," they will probably have trouble understanding each other. When the doctor tells his patient that she has "cholelithiasis," she probably would never guess that he means gallstones. When the lawyer tells his client that they need a "writ of certiorari," how is the client to know that it means they are going to appeal the case?

It's all just so much gobbledygook and bafflegab to other people. It's overcomplicated communications.

People in the military also use and abuse a jargon of their own. In fact, in 1977 the National Council of Teachers of English gave their Overall Doublespeak Award to the Pentagon for renaming the infamous neutron bomb, a "radiation enhancement weapon." The CIA ran a close second for calling its experiments in controlling human behavior "an investigation of human ecology." Sometimes jargon is deliberately used to confuse, and deliberate or not, it does confuse. And that is not usually the intention of human communication.

When we are talking to other people, whether in or outside our own profession or area of expertise, the shortest line between two points is still the straight one. The best way to communicate is the simplest, most straightforward way of expressing ourselves. In other words, the less time it takes to get both parties to the point, the better.

Of course, we don't mean to imply that everyone must speak in a dry, clipped, colorless style. What we mean is that we are all better understood when we simplify the message as much as possible, short of sterilizing it. Almost everyone can find ways to do that.

One way is just to ask yourself if you could say what you have to say in fewer words or in words that are less obscure. Think about the words you use, and if they don't do anything to help get your message across better, don't continue to use them. As it becomes more of a habit and you become more sensitive to those complicating words, it becomes easier to simplify.

Using Word Pictures

"To live long in politics you must possess the hide of a rhinoceros, the memory of an elephant, the persistence of a beaver, the native friendliness of a mongrel pup. You need the heart of a lion, and the stomach of an ostrich. And it helps to have the humor and ubiquity of a crow. But all of these combined are not enough, unless when you come to matters of principle, you also have the stubbornness of an army mule.''

This is Massachusetts Governor Robert Bradford's description of a successful politician. Now, everyone knows that a politician is not really a rhinoceros or an elephant or any of those other creatures Bradford compared them to. He was only using the comparisons to point out the likenesses under certain circumstances, to add color to what he was saying and to make it more meaningful to his audience. To see whether he succeeded, consider what his description would be like if he left out the comparisons.

Suppose that Governor Bradford had said instead, ''To live long in politics you must possess insensitivity to criticism, an excellent memory, persistence, friendliness and a strong stomach, and it helps to be good-natured and to have the ability to be everywhere at once. But all of these combined are not enough, unless when you come to matters of principle, you also have stubbornness.''

Which description do you think you would remember longer? Which speech would catch your attention and hold it?

There is an old saying that one picture is worth a thousand words. We think one word picture is worth ten thousand words. And the reason is that every descriptive word in a word picture, by conjuring up an *image* in the mind's eye of the listener, has double and sometimes even triple the effect.

''She was a cheerful, hearty soul and it was no more trouble for her to laugh than it is for a bird to sing.'' We can imagine this woman from the descriptive words of Mark Twain.

''There was freckled places on the ground where the light sifted down through the leaves, and the freckled places swapped about a little, showing there was a little breeze up there.'' Twain's description puts us there with Huckleberry Finn in a place much like one we have been to before and remember.

Many tools can be used to create word pictures. A speaker can use *analogy,* drawing explicit or implied comparisons. *Metaphors* can be used to create word pictures. You can also use *symbolism* and *allegory*. You can tell a narrative, an anecdote, a story, a tale, a yarn or give a report.

You can characterize. You can describe people, places and things. You are limited only by your imagination and by that of your listeners.

For more examples of word pictures you can look at any chapter in this book. Wherever there is an illustration or an analogy, an anecdote or an example, there is a word picture. It isn't always necessary to tell a whole story; expressive phrases, even single words may suffice. Any descriptive statement, phrase or word is a word picture if it increases the accuracy of perception of the listener.

If other people are able to get a picture in their minds of what you are talking about, then that makes what you are saying more appealing and interesting. The words that form vivid word pictures have a more lasting effect, because the picture will be retained long after the words have been forgotten.

Just Imagine!

As young James Watt sat before the fire, he whittled a cart out of wood and watched the lid of his grandmother's tea kettle being rattled and lifted by little puffs of steam. As he watched, he absentmindedly spun the wheels of the little cart.

"Grandmother," he said suddenly, "if the steam in the kettle is strong enough to lift the lid, why couldn't more steam lift heavier things or push wheels around?"

Robert Fulton had begun wondering, at the age of fourteen, if there couldn't be an easier way for men to move ships through water. First he made a model boat that was propelled by paddles at the sides. Then he designed a set of paddlewheels, which were joined by a bar and turned by a crank, which moved a scow through the water. Years later people lined the banks of the Hudson River to see the *Clermont* steam its way up-river.

Civilization itself is the product of creative thinking. The Renaissance was the result of a new attitude toward creativity. All the things since then that have provided us with the highest standard of living ever known—automobiles, railroads, airplanes, farm machinery, telephones, telegraph, television, electricity, air conditioning, wonder drugs, surgical procedures, walking on the moon—have been the results of creative thinking.

Training and education appear to have little to do with creativity. Samuel Morse, the inventor of the telegraph, was a portrait painter. Eli Whitney, the designer of the cotton gin, was a schoolteacher. Robert Moses, had he been the world's greatest engineer, could not have done more for New York City than he did with his creative approach to planning.

Creativity seeks to discover that which is new: new facts, new combinations, new possibilities, new applications. And the new is better if it solves problems.

Many retiring executives, by their own admission, have chosen their successors on the basis of the successor's creative approach to problems and ability to come up with new ideas. Even in social life the most attractive people are often the ones whose comments and conversations are more interesting because they are strictly and personally their own. Originality is attractive to us all.

Most of us were highly creative as children. But as we matured, we developed a list of things that work. We got into the habit of referring back to those things, never adding anything new, and stifling our creativity. We forgot how to ask ourselves the "what if" and "what else" questions, which produce the new idea or insight. But anyone can learn how to do that again. Everyone can reintroduce himself to his creative power.

If someone were to hand you a pencil and paper and ask you to write in thirty seconds a list of things to do if you were in your tenth-floor office and the building was about to fall down, you'd probably say, "I can't think of very many ideas that fast!" But if someone actually rushed into your office and shouted, "The building is going to fall down!" you would very quickly come up with some ideas on how to get out. The ideas are there and they will surface—when we allow them to.

To be more creative, temporarily tune out that part of your mind that is judgmental, that says, "It can't be done. It has never been done. There is no way to do it." The time for judgmental thinking is later, *after* the creative thinking is done. Judgment is confined to dealing with facts, and creativity requires reaching for the unknown. Judgment is often negative, but creativity thrives on a positive, optimistic outlook.

An example of the separation of creative and judgmental thinking is the story of Thomas Edison's first lamp. It was crude and imperfect, but he didn't hold onto it until he had perfected it, and he didn't throw it away. Imperfect as it was, it was still the best idea that anyone had ever had and better than anything else people were using for light at the time. So Edison introduced it, and then he went on to improve and perfect it.

Another good habit to develop is that of saying yes to new ideas. Like Edison, think of all the reasons an idea is good and should be tried. Think of all the possible new ideas and possible new approaches to a problem or project. Write them down even if they seem preposterous at the time, because many ideas prove to be more practical on second perusal than they may originally appear.

The main point is to set the imagination free. Other people will be judgmental enough; we don't have to pass judgment on our own ideas before we've even had a chance to try them out. That's like trying to get onto the expressway without taking your foot off the brake.

When we restrict ourselves to always doing or saying something in a certain way or to looking at problems from a certain viewpoint, just because that's the way we've always done it, we stifle creativity. How much better it is when people think up new approaches and present their opinions and viewpoints from a new perspective. The results are often pleasantly surprising, and so is the response.

One of the most precious gifts of nature is that each of us has a mind of his own. But like many other of our assets, we must either use it or lose it. Usually if we lose the ability to think creatively, it is by default. Creativity is like a muscle—it has to be stretched and exercised regularly to keep it fit and functioning.

So think your own thoughts and be an original. Take a chance on being different. Take a chance on yourself. Take a chance on being creative.

Don't Hedge

An overconscientious journalist was admonished by his editor, "Never write anything unless you are absolutely certain that it is true, and when you are not sure, say so very specifically."

The next story he turned in was a masterpiece of hedging. It read as follows: "It is rumored that a party was given yesterday by several reputed ladies. It was said that Mrs. Smith was the hostess and all the alleged guests were local people. Mrs. Smith claims to be the wife of Mr. Joseph Smith, who purports to be the president of the supposed First National Bank."

You can probably think of at least one experience you have had with someone who would never make a firm commitment to anything. He said things like, "Maybe we ought to buy that piece of machinery." Or "That's the best approach . . . I guess." Sometimes he acted as though he was all for it and ready to go ahead, but then there was always that *maybe* or *perhaps*. Almost everything he said had a question mark at the end of it, and people who had to deal with him were never sure about his position.

Harry H. broke his right wrist, and he was almost

completely incapacitated. He asked the doctor if there was anything he could do to help with the mending process. The doctor hemmed and hawed and finally said, "Oh, you might try exercising your hand." A month later Harry visited the doctor for his regular checkup. The cast was taken off the wrist, and Harry found he could not move his fingers. He was extremely upset, and so was the doctor.

"Haven't you been exercising every day?" asked the doctor.

"No, I didn't know it was necessary," Harry replied.

"I told you to exercise," the doctor said.

"You told me I might try exercising," Harry answered. "When you said *might* I assumed you didn't have much faith in the suggestion."

People often use hedging words unintentionally when they are trying to be polite. And sometimes it is just from habit that they say things like *maybe* or *I'm not sure, but* . . . Whatever the reason, what this actually could be communicating is an apparent lack of confidence in oneself. Using hedging terms could even be the reason the other person isn't willing to make a commitment. He can't feel confident about what we're saying if we don't sound confident ourselves. If we raise a question in his mind about our own commitment, then he is going to feel he has to be careful, too.

Beware of False Assumptions

Is the tall, handsome, athletic-looking man in the television commercial more masculine than was a gray-haired, aging Albert Schweitzer, who dedicated his life to helping humanity? Is the curvaceous, bosomy blonde with the come-hither smile more feminine than was Helen Keller, who was totally blind and deaf but who graduated cum laude from Radcliffe College and spent her entire life helping others overcome their handicaps?

Most of us would say no because we don't get taken in by that media hype. We would say that we don't judge people by superficial biological standards of how they look. We care about their human qualities and what they offer to others. We look beneath the surface of what they might seem to be and try to see what they really are. That's what most of us would say.

And yet human frailty will often lead us to assume that someone doesn't like us when he passes us in the hall and fails to say hello, even though there are any number of reasons someone might do that. Maybe he has a cold. Maybe he was distracted by another person he saw first. Maybe he was in deep thought about something else. Maybe we were outside his line of vision. But we immediately make the mistake of making a false assumption: he didn't say hello so he doesn't like me.

Making a false assumption is making a judgment without benefit of information. Making a false assumption about people means making a judgment about them, or about something they have done, before having made the effort to get all the information on which to base that judgment.

Sometimes we make false assumptions when, consciously or unconsciously, we pigeonhole, categorize or stereotype people or situations. Without having all the facts—without taking the time to check things out more thoroughly—we can make terrible mistakes.

For example, suppose a man says, "I'm tired of all this women's lib stuff. I think it's gone far enough." Someone hearing him might assume that he means that he is against women's rights. The other person might even resent what he said and accuse him of being a male chauvinist pig. But actually he could have said what he did for many reasons.

He could be reacting to being passed over for a promotion in favor of a woman with less seniority, by a company that wants to bring more women into upper management. Or he may be upset because his son couldn't get into the college of his choice, where the administration was filling a quota for women students. It could even mean that his wife is a member of NOW and is out picketing for women's rights, and he has to eat a TV dinner tonight, and besides . . . he hates to eat alone.

If he were given an opportunity to explain, he would probably have continued, "I'm all for women having equal rights, but . . . I wanted that job . . . My son deserved to go to that school . . . I hate TV dinners, and I miss my wife when she isn't home in the evenings."

Making false assumptions and reacting to them can be embarrassing to the assumer and devastating to relationships and careers. It is always worth the time and trouble to get the correct information, whatever it is. It's very easy to jump to a conclusion and make a false assumption, but the jump could end at the bottom of the ladder of success.

Humor Opens Doors

When Carolyn first went into business, a representative of a large company called her to say he would be in town on a certain day and would attend a seminar she had scheduled. Carolyn looked at the schedule and told him with some trepidation, "I don't have a seminar scheduled for that day."

"What do you mean, you don't have a seminar that day?" he asked angrily. "I have the schedule right here before me, and it says that you do. I've already made arrangements to attend and to bring someone with me." After a moment's pause he continued more calmly, "All right, let's see what else we can do. I'm looking at your schedule and you have another seminar on the following Monday, which will be just as good for me. I'll see if I can make the arrangements for that time."

Carolyn looked at the schedule again and didn't see a seminar on that day, either. When she told him, there was a long silence on the telephone before he said in an angry voice, "What kind of a businesswoman are you?"

"Lousy," she said. "But doesn't that tell you something about my seminars? If I'm such a terrible businesswoman and yet my seminars have gotten such a great reputation, I must be doing *something* right!"

He laughed. Then Carolyn told him that she had apparently made a mistake and sent him last year's schedule and that she would send him a current schedule immediately. As a result of that encounter, he has been a steady client ever since. During times of pressure or crisis, especially in business, a little humor can often save everyone's sanity, as well as saving the day.

Humor can soften a blow to self-esteem or pride. Our capacity to laugh at ourselves and to help others laugh at themselves can be a kind of protective barrier between success and failure. Humor makes problem solving much easier because it makes the other person more receptive to what you are saying and brings you both closer together and closer to agreement. People can't laugh and feel negative or angry at the same time.

Every day each of us has to face life anew. Every day we have to get out of bed, recharge our batteries and take on the challenges and pitfalls, promises and pain ahead of us. Anytime someone helps us laugh and feel better, we have a more appreciative attitude toward that person. Humor makes both the givers and the receivers feel better. It's as simple as that.

Laughter works by removing negativism, putting people in a frame of mind that makes them more responsive to you and ready for positive ideas. When peole are in this optimistic mood, they will naturally view your ideas through that positive, optimistic viewpoint. That is not to say they will lose their wits and blindly agree to whatever you say; only that they will begin from a more accepting stance.

Make people laugh, and they will like you more for it. Make them see the humor in a situation, and they will be grateful to you. And then when you have their attention, tell them what you want them to hear. They will be much more receptive.

Animate Your Face and Voice

There is a computer that can perform twelve million functions per second. The human mind cannot approach that capacity. But only the human mind was able to conceive and construct the computer. No matter how marvelous a computer may be, even the most limited human being has a mind that can do what a computer cannot do, like imagine things and feel emotion.

Yet some people go to work every day as if they were going to a kind of masquerade. Each morning they put on their disguises, which they feel shield them from others. They could spend their entire day with other people who never really learn what is behind the disguise.

The masks they wear are protective devices they have learned to use from experience. We all learn to mask ourselves while we are growing up, as we learn to hide some of our feelings or modify them. It's a necessary part of the civilizing process, and to a certain extent there's nothing wrong with protecting ourselves. In certain situations, business as well as social, it's wise to mask our feelings. If we don't like the boss but there is no other job available to us right now, it's wise to hide our dislike. It's essential to survival. Being totally uninhibited can cost us a job. And there are other situations where we could be exposed to criticism, embarrassment or censure.

But we wear many different kinds of masks, and too often we wear them without realizing that we don't need them. When we do that, those masks can also overprotect us from engaging in the give-and-take of the business world. And if we don't give, we can't get.

Wearing a mask over your personality cuts off open communication and destroys any chance of real friendship. It's a kind of personal censorship that, like other kinds of censorship, takes out the most interesting parts. In communicating with others, it is the sharing of our *selves*—of what we know, of what we think and of what we feel—that makes us interesting to others.

The person who never unmasks to reveal his feelings is building a barrier between himself and other people. That wall can become a kind of prison for him, locking him away from success.

There is usually no real reason for people to hide from each other as much as some do, because no one is perfect. By holding back animation, we just make ourselves wooden puppets who are only going through the motions with a pasted-on false face.

There are lots of excuses: "I'm not an emotional person." "I'm not a good speaker." "I'm not articulate." But by taking off the masks, we can enjoy being ourselves. Anyone can learn to let go a little, a little at a time. Try it. The next time you're preparing to speak, try to inject a little more spontaneity into the words. Have some idea of what you're going to say, but don't rehearse all the spontaneity out of it.

Try being less self-critical. Self-criticism can squash all the spontaneity—and the fun—out of speaking. Try to feel more self-accepting and less worried about looking or sounding foolish. Enthusiasm is contagious and if you're lively, you'll be hard to resist.

Look people in the eye and they'll look back, and it won't be hard to convince them that you mean what you say. Because when you say, "Joe, that was a great presentation," you'll look and sound as though you really mean it.

Almost every spoken communication can have more than one meaning. The listener can become confused, or if he's forced to make an interpretation, might make the wrong one. If we want the other person to respond to our message, he has to know what it really is.

For example, if someone says, "The old hometown certainly has changed," without any revealing animation about whether he thinks it is for better or worse, how is the listener to know? How is he to respond?

We don't mean to imply that anyone should try to express a feeling that he doesn't really feel. No one can make himself feel what he does not, and no one should pretend otherwise. But *animation*, the open expression of what we are really feeling, adds another dimension to communications.

How we say what we say tells the other person what we are feeling about him, how we feel about what we're talking about and how we feel about ourselves at the moment. But besides all that, animation of the face and voice makes what we are saying that much more interesting.

Making a Commitment

Andrew Carnegie, the great industrialist and philanthropist, once declared in a speech before a graduating class that he thought all young men fell into three categories: those who did not do all their duty, those who only professed to do their duty and those who did their duty plus "a little more."

"It is the little more that wins," he said. "Do your duty and the little more, and the future will take care of itself."

His own life story is an example of what Carnegie was talking about. At the tender age of ten, he went to work as a bobbin boy for $1.20 a week. His commitment took him upward through a succession of positions, from assistant to the factory engineer to telegraph boy to telegraph operator. By copying telegrams for the newspaper, he earned a dollar a week extra, which he invested in the express business, then in sleeping cars and finally in a plant that manufactured railway bridges.

Not everyone in business can expect to be an Andrew Carnegie, any more than every psychiatrist can be a Freud or every mathematician an Einstein. Nature endows each of us with different abilities, capacities and interests. But if we set goals for ourselves that are reasonable and that we can realistically expect to achieve —and make that *full commitment* to them—we can expect to have a higher rate of success.

The history of the business world is filled with the exciting success stories of people who could commit themselves to goals for themselves and the people who worked for them, and whose commitment to those goals helped them surmount obstacles that stood between them and the accomplishment of those goals. Harlow Curtice was one of those people. He had grown up in a rural part of the country and his education had gone no further than a high-school diploma. In 1914 he got a job as a bookkeeper with a subsidiary of General Motors. By the time he was thirty-five years old, he had become president of the company, and by the time he was forty, he had become the general manager of General Motors' Buick Division. During that time he was responsible for bringing about some daring changes in design as well as having revised the Buick sales channels. He traveled around the country personally to visit the numerous Buick dealerships and promote faith in the product. Because of Curtice's total commitment, sales of Buick automobiles quadrupled to become General Motors' second biggest source of earnings. And he did all this during the middle four years of the economic depression of the 1930s.

This country's history has been made by people who had a firm commitment and who stuck to their guns. We all have to make commitments every day in our personal lives—to sweethearts, spouses, children, family members and friends. You had to make a commitment when you decided to become an organized listener. It's the same thing in business.

One day a memorandum from the office manager was distributed to everyone on the third floor of Boscumb and Bartlett Design Engineers. It began, "Subject: Need for a more professional attitude on the Third Floor." Then it read, "It has come to my attention that there may be some misunderstanding of this company's standard of professionalism. In view of this, it would be to each person's advantage to consider and become aware of the condition and appearance of his own work area and immediate surroundings. I am especially concerned about the impression we make on visiting customers, and I expect everyone to comply."

The next day, neatly attired in coats and ties, the men of the third floor were startled to see the office manager appear in a sports coat and cardigan sweater. Obviously he hadn't totally committed *himself* to the new professionalism. That's not very good management, and it's extremely poor communication.

If you're going to do something, do it the best you can. Commit yourself wholly and completely, and then follow through a hundred percent.

The Main Responsibility Is with the Sender

Ben was preparing his favorite breakfast of hot oatmeal when his daughter came rushing in with his little grandson Tommy.

"The baby-sitter has been delayed," she explained, "and I've got to go to work. Will you keep Tommy for a few hours?"

Ben said sure and his daughter left. Then Ben scooped up two bowls of oatmeal. "Do you like sugar?" he asked Tommy.

Tommy nodded.

"How about some butter, too?"

Again his grandson nodded.

"Of course you like milk?"

"Sure," the boy said.

But when Ben placed the steaming bowl of oatmeal with sugar, butter, and milk before Tommy, the boy made a face and pushed it away.

"Don't want it," he said, making another face.

"But when I asked you, you said you liked sugar, butter and milk," Ben protested.

"Yeah," Tommy answered, "but you didn't ask me if I like oatmeal."

No matter how carefully you prepare, no matter how well it seems to be going, the communication isn't finished until the last words have been said, the last bit of feedback given and received and an agreement reached.

And the main responsibility is with the sender. You should bear that responsibility well when it falls to you.

All of us know what it means to take responsibility. We take responsibility for many things in every aspect of our lives, from doing the yard work to keeping the checkbook balanced. And just as we hold up our end of the responsibility at home and in our relationships with our family and friends, we have the responsibility for communicating on the job or in our place of business, for seeing that we send messages clearly and comprehensibly and in an interest-catching way. We can't depend on others to take the responsibility for what we are saying to them. It isn't theirs to take, and we will be disappointed again and again if we expect that.

Effective and successful communication has taken place when the person to whom we are sending our message has received and interpreted it exactly as we meant it. The responsibility obviously lies with the person *sending* the message, because it contains his own ideas, feelings and intentions.

No matter how good a listener the receiver is—no matter how much discipline and skill he has—he can only receive what is being sent. So when you are the sender in a communication, take that responsibility. Use all the techniques you have learned that can help you, and give it your best effort every time.

An Exercise

Every once in a while, especially in business, you run across someone with whom you seem to have all kinds of communication difficulties. You do all the things you ordinarily do, but you just can't seem to get past that invisible barrier. And you wish you could think of something new to try, because it is very important that you get your message across.

In our seminars we have people complete an exercise

that involves dealing with communications barriers to see whether they are able to get their messages past a *real* barrier and how they do it. We are including the exercise here for you to try. In it you will communicate a drawing to your partner, and have your partner draw it according to your description. We wish to point out that the exercise is not a test of artistic ability. The aim is not to find out how well you can sketch but to demonstrate how the techniques of effective communication can help even under the most trying conditions.

Here is the step-by-step way to do the exercise.

1. Find someone to be your partner. The partner could be a friend, a family member or anyone who is willing to help you do this exercise.
2. The "tools" for this exercise will be this book, a large folder or loose-leaf notebook or another book the same size or larger, a pencil and an eraser, some unmarked and unlined sheets of typewriter paper and a narrow table and two chairs.
3. In the center of the table, set up the large book as a barrier that will stand between you and your partner when you sit at the table. Make sure that neither of you will be able to see over it when it stands upright between you. In other words, it should be tall enough so that you cannot see the paper in front of your partner and your partner cannot see the drawing in the book in front of you.
4. Place the pencil, eraser and paper on the table on one side of the barrier, and place this book on the other side of the barrier. Ask your partner to sit on the side that has the pencil, eraser and paper. You will sit on the side that has this book.
5. Set a time limit for yourselves to complete the exercise. We suggest any time between fifteen and twenty minutes. This is the part of the exer-

cise where you can practice the technique of *having a sense of urgency*. The length of the time limit itself is not as important as the decision to set one, because without a time limit, the exercise might never be finished.

6. Now you are ready to begin. Your part of the exercise is to describe to your partner the drawing in the book at the end of this chapter on page 190, so that your partner can draw it by following your verbal description. Here are some guidelines that you can follow:

Think of an *overview* of what you see, and then use *word pictures* to communicate that. For instance, does it remind you of a sunrise or sunset on two mountaintops? Do you see a large letter Z? Or a snake that is carrying away an orange? Tell your partner, taking one thing at a time, being specific and using simple words and sentences.

Next describe the dimensions of the drawing. For example, is there as much space at the top as at the bottom? Once you have determined the dimensions, tell your partner. You might find it helpful if you choose as an example an object you can both see. For instance, you might say, "It looks about the length of your pencil" or "It is six-sided like that ashtray." Since you are communicating verbally only, not using your hands to describe size, such comparisons can be helpful.

Your partner may ask anything he wants to about the drawing or about what you say. For example, if you say, "It looks like a snake," your partner might ask, "Is it a skinny snake or a fat snake?" The giving and receiving of this kind of feedback will help you both clarify the messages.

We suggest to people that if they finish before their time is up, they might want to go through the exercise again, summarizing, talking to each other about it and asking the partner questions about what he did. Many people think they are finished before they have *reviewed*. Frequently, after they have taken just a few minutes to go over it again, they find they can make a little change that makes a big difference.

If you're not finished when the time limit has expired, don't worry. Remember, this is strictly an exercise in verbal communications to see the methods by which you can get a message across when there is a barrier in your way, not how fast you can do it.

When you have finished, have a discussion with your partner about what you have accomplished. You will become much more aware of how you communicate with others, and that insight can be invaluable to you.

Participants in the seminar discover that the same word does not always mean the same thing to all people. We once had an older gentleman sitting across from a younger woman, and the woman described something as looking like a Slinky, a popular toy for children. Afterward the man looked at the original drawing and said to her, "Honey, that's not *my* idea of slinky."

Generally people will manage to find a common ground with which they can both work. And usually the exercise makes them think of some other good communications techniques. They become aware of some of the techniques they have used as well as some of the ones they haven't used.

This exercise may remind you of trying to communicate clearly over the telephone. You have probably found that when you're on the phone and can't see the other person or use your hands, communication is more difficult. Sometimes you use your hands even though they can't be seen, as if to convince yourself of something. We are all so accustomed to depending on hand movements to help us convey meaning that it's very hard not to use them. But they're not helpful at all when the other person can't see what you are indicating, and so you are forced to find other ways to express yourself. You have to become more creative in your communication with the other party.

Without being able to see the other person, you are deprived of some other kinds of feedback you usually rely upon, such as body language, eye contact and facial expression. These can tell you a great deal about what the other person is actually hearing and how he is interpreting it. Many persons who depend exclusively on the telephone for business communications, such as telephone salespeople, use a mirror. Seeing their own image causes them to animate more, and that animation can be transmitted verbally. This may increase the personal animation, but you are still deprived of visual feedback. Then giving and receiving verbal feedback becomes even more important. What happens too often is that when either person has said something that apparently wasn't understood by the other, the speaker's voice gets louder, as if saying something louder will get the message across better. Instead, speak explicitly and don't rely on slang and other easily misconstrued words and phrases. You have to find more than one way to express things, more than one way to explain. That's not easy. But if you can go in more than one direction, the perceptions of the other person can be much more accurate. And you can be more creative using word pictures to reinforce what you are saying.

We have stated throughout this book our belief that good communication is a two-way, act/react situation, because we want you to be as aware of this as we are. We think that by having experience with it yourself, as through this communications-barrier exercise, you will have learned more about how you communicate. And you will have helped someone you know learn more about how he or she communicates. And that sharing and exchanging, giving and getting, is in a nutshell what good communicating is basically all about.

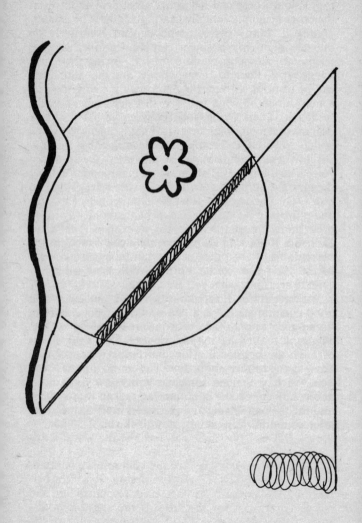

· 22 ·
Self-Image
(Don't Sit on Your Assets)

There are those who allow personal achievement to remain an elusive dream because their self-image is inaccurately perceived and therefore of little practical use to them in life. *Self-image sets the boundaries of individual accomplishments.* We promise according to our hopes (the kind of person we'd like to believe we could become) and perform according to our fears (the kind of person we're inclined to think we are). That's the reality of it. That's the point at which most of us unconsciously allow it to rest. We're not really sure how to proceed from there. We see the facade in many of the situations and circumstances of life, and we realize it may be a disguise the world wears to disconcert the timid. But we are hesitant because we so often lack the self-image— the confidence—to reach out and test the world's disguise.

Too often we don't try for the committee chairmanship; don't go after the opportunities we see for the better job, the position of increased responsibility and reward; don't ask for the raise. If the world *is* in disguise, if that disguise is a bluff to scare us off, we too often accept the bluff and fold our hands without asking to see the cards this masked player is actually holding. He looks so confident in his disguise, and we are too easily intimidated by it.

The world belongs to the confident. That statement is not the revelation of some great, carefully guarded secret; it is a fact that successful people in every walk of life, throughout every period of time, have proved over and over again. Knowing yourself—knowing what you have to offer—is the key.

How can you locate that self-confident person you'd like to become? The adventure of finding that person within yourself necessarily begins with a little believing, a little realistic positive thinking.

The fact is that none of us is perfect. We all know that. If we are ever in danger of forgetting it, our parents, our teachers, our spouses, often even our bosses and our children are always glad to remind us how imperfect we are. Self-improvement, a confident self-image and hope for the future do not come from trying to tell yourself you are perfect. You *know* it ain't so.

But a realistically positive approach, using the practical aspects of positive thinking, can improved both your own self-image and the way you deal with others. Our concept is simply to minimize your liabilities and maximize your assets, and to try to do the same for everyone around you.

Everyone is already skilled at finding fault. None of us needs any extracurricular training in that. You could probably think of six bad names to call your teenage son in a matter of seconds. However, since the whole individual consists of faults *and* assets, it only makes sense to exercise our capacity for finding the good in people. This is a faculty some of us use so seldom that we may have a hard time warming it up and getting it to work properly.

This doesn't mean you have to go around murmuring blessings on everybody or suddenly become a Pollyanna, so thankful for life's tiniest favors that you feel obligated to say, "Yes, the bus did run over my foot, but isn't it lucky that Uncle Joe rents hospital appliances and I got my crutches at a discount?'' What we're suggesting is simply that you concentrate on assets—your own and the other fellow's—instead of faults, and let that work for you. To begin with, look for the best in yourself. If you don't think well of yourself, no one else will. But if you steadily project an affirmative image of yourself in your own mind, you will indeed become more like that image.

Picture yourself about to present a description of your company's services to a prospective customer; or maybe it's your turn to give the monthly book review to The Guild; or you're about to deliver a report on the finances of your local civic club or charitable organization. You have a choice. You can either maximize the picture of your assets at work or you can focus on your faults. You can either imagine yourself shaking so hard you knock over the glass of water near your elbow, crumpling tissues to bits in your sweaty palm and stuttering so badly over the first words that it takes you five minutes to complete the first sentence, or you can concentrate on an affirmative mental picture of yourself: poised, smiling, well groomed, confidently delivering your remarks with the polish of a pro. Of course, self-confidence will be born, realistically, out of preparation and practice. A positive mental image is another step in the preparation of the completely confident self-image.

· 23 ·
Application for Success
(See Attached)

The world we live in is full of possibility, opportunity—
and paperwork. For every opportunity, it seems, there is
a form to be filled out. In many cases these forms are
designed to "formulate" people and their abilities into
categories—the qualified and the unqualified, the "in"
basket or the "out" basket. Occasionally a highly qualified applicant doesn't exactly fit these formula slots and
must find a way to redirect a potential employer's attention.

One woman did exactly this. She shared her personal
experience during one of our seminars. We call her story
"See Attached."

After fifteen years of professional experience and
wide acceptance as an authority in her field (journalism
and publishing), this woman happened to see an ad in
the local paper for instructors for a new community college due to open in the fall. At this point in her career,
she felt she had a wealth of practical experience to offer
in these related and overlapping subjects and, further,
that she could now afford to devote a portion of her
time to working with aspiring writers. The dean of the

college mailed her an application, but when it arrived, she was not surprised to find that almost the entire first page was a maze of lines, boxes and spaces to be filled in regarding "Education." She had nothing to fill in that fit the lines, boxes and spaces. She had had no formal education past high school. Due to the unusual circumstances of her life, she had never had a single hour of formal, college-classroom study.

Although an articulate and well-educated person, the problem was, as it always had been, that her education simply didn't fit the slots of conformity the world expected. After completing the usual chronological listing of staff and editorial positions she had held, further publishing credits, awards and professional career affiliations, she turned back to the Education page, drew a long diagonal slash across the lines and boxes, and wrote: "See Attached."

In an attached letter she offered a brief, conversational summary of her accumulated private studies over the years, both in terms of specific subject matter and the humanities. Citing the fact that her personal background included wide travel in the United States, the Orient and Mexico, she counted these broadening experiences as a valuable part of her education as a writer and as a person. Noting that she had first been published at the age of thirteen, she went on to say that "the best education for a writer is *to write,* and good writing can blossom from every endeavor and life experience. But the best writing experience is to be *published*, and that will be my goal for each student in the course I have outlined. My own years spent professionally in the career of writing and editing now give me the opportunity to offer new and hopeful writers a specific study and practical application of the craft, as well as confidence, motivation and sincere empathy with their efforts."

She got the job. She has now added three years of successful teaching to her resumé—which still does not fit the slots of a formula application for success.

There are many areas in life where a labor of love

in the pursuit of knowledge on a subject can and frequently does turn into an impressive education. Perhaps one of the most important elements that comes with this kind of private study is emotion: the special emotional ingredients of enthusiasm and desire to learn, for pleasure. Most of the "application forms" in life offer no line or space for information regarding special enthusiasms or desires or knowledge. Paperwork is limited to facts, while a great deal in life is accomplished through creative imagination and its application to opportunity.

For instance, a good many men have imagined that they might become president of the United States. It could certainly be agreed that in America one of the most significant qualifications for the office of presidency is charisma, that certain subtle combination of communication ingredients that give a candidate public appeal.

But where would you list that on an application form? Just for a moment try to imagine that there is a written application form for the job called president of the United States, and that no media are allowed in the game. Just as when most of us apply for a job, there will be no stories in the newspapers amplifying our opinions. There will be no media blitz to display to the boss that one of our assets is a pleasant, well-groomed appearance and a dynamite smile. In this game you just come in during office hours at the White House and fill out an application for the job, like everyone else. Just sign it at the bottom and leave a number where you can be reached.

Some of those applications would have read along these lines:

Background: Born in a log cabin. I have had extensive but informal study. Good ideas.
—Signed, A. Lincoln
Previous occupation: Peanut farmer. I have an intense desire to be president. Good teeth.
—Signed, J. Carter

Primary job skill: Actor. I have played a wide
variety of parts, which has given me the ability
to appear to be whatever seems most appropriate to the situation at hand. Good hair.
—Signed, R. Reagan

The field of politics, from the local to the national
level, is based entirely on the philosophy of "listen to
attached." "I know what it says on my application,
but just listen to my other assets, my ideas, my addi-
tional qualifications—hear what I have to tell you that
wouldn't fit on the lines and spaces of your application
form."

There is no such thing as "an unqualified success."
Everyone who aspires to or achieves success of any kind
had specific, occasionally unique qualifications and
assets that have been developing and accumulating
throughout his or her lifetime. And that includes you.

All too often in life your unique combination of qualifications and assets, so applicable to the opportunity,
simply does not fit the lines and spaces of the application form. That is when you need to consider drawing
interest on those accumulated assets in your bank of experience or, perhaps, drawing more interest and attention to those assets in the many applications of life.

Never underestimate the fact that the experience and
assets you've been accumulating throughout your life,
as well as your specific job skills or degrees, are invaluable in the world of business. Business itself is a whole
world of interaction between people, daily relationships, ideas, communications—not just products, plans
and paperwork. If and when it seems appropriate to the
situation, make an opportunity to direct a potential employer's attention to you. As just one example among
many, do you have the personal confidence and sense of
caring to motivate other people to their best efforts?
These qualities happen to be assets, abilities not usually
allowed for on applications, which business is discovering to be specifically important factors in management
and leadership.

It is widely agreed that two of Henry Ford's finest assets in business were his ability to organize and his ability to delegate. There is seldom a line, space or box on an application asking, "Do you understand the importance of organization and delegation? Do you consider yourself competent in these areas?"

In fact, it was primarily these two abilities that enabled him to dispel once and for all the label of ignorance some of his contemporaries had tried to pin on him. The story is told, based on fact, that during the First World War a Chicago newspaper had published some unflattering editorials about Ford, at one point calling him an "ignorant pacifist." It was generally known that Henry Ford had little formal education, and it was therefore often mistakenly assumed that he was ignorant.

Ford subsequently sued the newspaper for libel. In an effort to prove that he was indeed an ignorant man, the attorney for the newspaper placed Mr. Ford himself on the witness stand. Possibly in the hope of provoking an "ignorant" display of temper and a variety of foolish responses, all manner of slightly inane questions were thrown at him—none of them, of course, having to do with the manufacture of automobiles, a subject on which he was obviously well informed. Newspaper accounts report that one of the questions asked was, "How many soldiers did the British send over to America to put down the rebellion of 1776?" To which Mr. Ford is said to have replied, "I do not know the exact number of soldiers the British sent over, but I have heard that it was a considerably larger number than ever went back."

Finally, tiring of the offensive line of questioning, Ford leaned forward in a rather aggressive posture and interrupted the proceedings with this:

"If I really wanted to answer any of your foolish questions, let me remind you that by pushing the correct button on my desk, I have men at my disposal who can answer any question concerning the business to which I am devoting my efforts. Now, please tell me why I should clutter up my mind with trivial general knowledge for the purpose of being able to answer questions, when I have surrounded myself with men who can supply any knowledge I require?''

The simple logic of Ford's response seemed obvious to everyone in the courtroom. It was not the answer of an ignorant man. If Henry Ford had found it necessary to apply for his success, on paper, it seems certain that somewhere on that application he would have written: "See Attached.''

In most of the world's "applications for success," most of its possibilities and opportunities, the fact remains that who's qualified and who's not is usually decided by someone other than ourselves. An opinion must be reached at some point. The problem, perhaps, is that most of us become used simply to accepting someone else's opinion of our qualifications without question.

Ford might have been intimidated into accepting someone else's opinion that he was an ignorant man. He did not allow that to happen. Instead he held that his own opinion of himself was more important than someone else's.

"Know thyself," admonished a Delphic Oracle inscription, as have countless generations since. And yet many people are held back from speaking the language of success by fear of how to begin that complex journey into the unknown, that search for ourselves, for that hidden voice of confidence somewhere within.

In our concept—one that has proven successful for our thousands of seminar participants for over a decade —we begin to move toward the confident self-image by asking everyone to list his or her most valuable assets *as a human being*. These can be anything from intelligence to personality traits like charm, courtesy or thoughtfulness, to appearance, to character traits like courage or perseverance, or the ability to work with others and dependability. Anything goes.

We're going to ask you to write down your best assets here. This is your own road map, to be referred to and

used long after you've closed the covers of this book.
We call this your "See Attached" list:

_____

_____

_____

_____

_____

   Be affirmative and fair with yourself. Never mind if
your mother spent the last five years of your life at
home telling you that you're not as smart as your
brother, or your spouse tells you that you never get
anything done. You're looking for the personal picture
you have in your own mind of your best self. Don't sit
on your assets!
   The next guidepost on your map, the follow-up step,
is to ask the same question of others. What "See Attached" qualities or assets do you see in me as a human
being? And these are the others to ask:

1. Your boss or immediate supervisor at work
2. Your spouse (or a close friend or parent if
   you're not married)
3. Any child in your family over five years old
   (your own child, a niece or nephew, etc.)
4. A relatively new acquaintance

   For some people this is the most difficult assignment
they have ever had. In everyone, no matter how apparently secure, there lurks the secret fear that your husband, wife, children, friends or boss may not be able to
think of five nice things to say about you. Or that they
may hem and haw embarrassedly. At which point you
visualize yourself having to say, "Aw, never mind. Just
skip it." That never, ever happens. But do give your
respondents overnight to collect their thoughts about
you, to consider what they really know and feel about
you. Give them a chance to be fair. Tell them it's part of
a communications experiment you're conducting or

anything else believable if you're hesitant about how to approach them. But be sure you get serious answers, not facetious ones.

Don't cheat on yourself. Do this *for yourself!* We promise you, you will be amazed at the results. Your self-esteem, and with it your confidence, will rise several degrees.

After you've gathered all your "other" lists together, sit down in a quiet moment, in a quiet place, and enter those lists of assets other people found in you here in your book, as:

"See Attached"/As Others See Me:
  (Be sure to vary the headings we've given here to indicate the actual people you asked. In the months and years to come, you will want to remember exactly who they were.)

Boss/   Spouse/Close Friend/
Supervisor: Parent:

_____   _____
_____   _____
_____   _____
_____   _____

Child: Acquaintance/Co-worker:

_____   _____
_____   _____
_____   _____
_____   _____

You will find it fascinating to compare your own description of yourself with what others see in you. The discrepancies will be as interesting as the similarities.

Initially, when most people are asked to write their own "See Attached" list of assets, embarrassment and

reluctance are strong. Some of us feel almost guilty if
anyone compliments us or so embarrassed that we ignore it. Worse, we often unconsciously offend the person who complimented us by making an inept and in-
secure response.

Knowing your assets doesn't mean you have to go
around bragging about them, certainly, but it's the
essential basis of self-knowledge, of who you really are.
Self-knowledge is the very heart of self-confidence, and
confidence is the heart of successful verbal communication, of speaking the language of success in every situation in life.

Often people discover that a characteristic they
thought of as a liability is perceived as an asset by everyone else. In one seminar group a woman bank teller with
a sweet smile learned, to her shock, that people interpreted her "quiet" as pleasant calm and felt the room
was the nicer for her presence even when she didn't say a
word!

"I was a middle child," she confided, "and my older
sister was very outgoing and was always putting me
down because I couldn't come out of my shell." Although she described herself as being too reserved, too
much of a loner, other people saw a relaxed, calm
woman who emanated warmth and caring before she
ever opened her mouth.

There's no need to waste time rationalizing away your
liabilities. On balance, they're just *there*. You know
what they are. Now stop dwelling on them; minimize
your liabilities. Change the emphasis of your thinking.
Concentrate on what you like and what others like
about you. Use that as a point of reference in finding
and building your awareness and confidence.

If you are one of the untold numbers of people who
share the characteristic of shyness or timidity, relax and
realize that you can change those feelings. You're not
saddled with them for life. No one handed out those
feelings in the first round of cards and said you were
stuck with them. Discard them and draw from your
deck of assets. Insist on recognizing the value in your-

self. That's confidence. You can *make* yourself a confident person.

No rose-colored glasses, no rose garden of wishful thinking. Just an affirmative, confident knowledge of yourself. The world does belong to the confident, as you'll discover.

·24·
Using the Assets of Others
(Winning Ways)

Joanna D. was driving home from work when a woman in another car began honking at her and shouting for Joanna to pull over. Joanna drove her car onto the shoulder of the road and stopped, and the other driver pulled up alongside. But when Joanna rolled down the window, the other woman unexpectedly began to shout obscenities at her. Naturally Joanna didn't feel she should just sit there and take abuse, so she rolled up the window and drove on.

But in just a few minutes she realized that the other person was following her and making angry gestures. Then the angry woman in the other car started pulling close to Joanna's car, acting as though she was deliberately going to bump fenders. Joanna was beginning to be frightened by the wild behavior of the other driver, and she made a quick decision to seek safety in a nearby shopping center. But before she could get out of her car and into the haven of the supermarket, the other car pulled up behind her and the incensed woman got out and came toward her, still shouting threats.

Joanna had never seen anyone behaving this way and

had never been attacked with such a string of epithets. She wasn't sure what she should do as the other woman continued to advance angrily toward her.

Then as the woman reached her side, Joanna said firmly, "Miss, I appreciate that you stopped to talk with me. I must have inadvertently done something awful to have gotten you as upset as you are. I must have almost had a terrible accident that I wasn't aware of. But I really do admire you for taking all this time to bring it to my attention. I think it shows that you are a very alert driver and very conscious of the way accidents can happen."

The other woman looked at Joanna for a moment, then said, "Well, just be more careful."

By looking at the reverse side of the other driver's anger, Joanna revealed an asset, appealed to the better nature of the angry woman and defused a very volatile situation.

Joanna, like most of us, likes to think of herself as sensitive to the point of view of others. She knows this trait is an asset, and that when she uses her assets, she lives up to the best within herself. She also knows that when she can show others their assets, she helps them live up to the best within themselves. By using assets she keeps control of touchy situations, turning them into more positive experiences for everyone involved. She uses assets to motivate people to more desirable behavior.

To manage and interact with other people, we also have to do something for other people. We believe that one of the greatest things you can do for others is motivate them, reinforce them and help them live up to the best of what others see in them. From knowing what it feels like to be told our assets and from having the wonderful experience of dealing with our own assets, it is a logical progression to dealing with other people in the same manner.

Of course, it takes effort and practice to nurture an attitude of seeing assets rather than pointing out liabilities, of complimenting rather than complaining, of praising rather than criticizing, because in this imperfect world of imperfect people, it is always easier to find things to criticize than things to praise. But the payoff is worth the effort, because for you, as a true believer in the positive power of asset awareness, there will always be a better way of saying something that will help you make a friend, please a spouse, raise a child or manage a career.

Joe B. and his wife, Marta, were the caring and concerned parents of a rebellious teenage son, David, with whom they were having many conflicts. Joe was a highly successful man who had become president of his own firm by the time he was forty; he was obviously a person who knew and understood the principles of successful communication. When he and Marta attended one of our seminars, Joe seemed to be somewhat uninterested in hearing things he already knew. But Marta said to him, "You know, this assets technique sounds inordinately simple. Since we've tried everything else with David, why don't we try this?"

A year later we saw Joe and Marta again, and they eagerly told us what had happened in their family. "We realized that we had been saying things to David like, 'You have a lot of potential but you're not living up to it,' and 'It breaks our hearts to see you achieve so little when we know you are so intelligent,' " Marta said. "We saw that we were always giving him criticism with the compliments. 'You are a thoughtful young man . . . when you choose to be.' 'You are very charming . . . when you make the effort.' So whenever we caught ourselves doing that, we stopped, and then said only the positive part. We said, 'You have a gift for drawing people out . . .' and stopped. We said, 'You have a great ability to concentrate . . .' and stopped. We used no more *but*s.

"It has taken a lot of time and effort for us to separate our compliments from the criticisms, but it has been well worth it," Marta said with a smile. "We have our boy back, and we are communicating like a family again."

When children are raised with their assets emphasized instead of their liabilities, lots of interesting things happen. Elaine R. had applied for a summer job to earn some money before returning to college in the fall semester. She was making a good impression, the interview seemed to be going very well, and when the interviewer asked Elaine what she thought her assets were, Elaine zipped them right off.

"I'm very responsible, and I'm thoughtful of others, and I'm very creative," Elaine said confidently.

"I see," the interviewer said slowly, somewhat taken aback because she had never before heard anyone do that quite as easily. "All right, now tell me, what are your liabilities?" There was a long silence.

Finally Elaine said, "I told you that I'm very conscientious. Well, sometimes I'm obsessive and really work too hard. And I told you that I care about other people. Well, sometimes I take that to extremes and I care too much. And I told you that I'm creative. Well, sometimes I think an awful lot and come up with some unusual solutions to problems." The postscript to this story is that, of course, Elaine got the job.

Although there is just as much reason for people to emphasize each other's assets after marriage, somehow many forget that there is still that need. It may be because they feel they can take each other for granted or they think that he or she has been told enough times to know.

Meg N. attended our seminar. She had the usual assignment of obtaining a list of her five greatest assets from her husband for her "See Attached" list. She turned to her husband of twelve years and said, "Honey, tell me what you think my five greatest assets are."

Albert put down the medical journal he was reading and, smiling mischievously, he said, "I am."

"Please, be serious," Meg coaxed. "I really want to know what you think my assets are. For instance, I can tell you that I think one of your greatest assets is . . ." Meg paused thoughtfully, and Albert became curious and more attentive. ". . . is that when you perform surgery on someone, you don't just see that person as a 'case.' You see real people, and you treat them with dignity and even love. And I think that's one of your greatest assets."

"Do you really think so?" Albert asked, obviously moved.

"Oh, yes, I always have," Meg replied.

After a moment Albert said, "Why haven't you ever told me that before?"

Meg thought to herself, Shouldn't he have known? After all these years isn't it logical that he would know how I feel? Then she answered simply, "I don't know why I never told you before."

Albert told Meg what he saw as her five greatest assets, and among them was, "You are a very understanding wife." Meg was surprised, so Albert elaborated. "When I was going through my surgical residency and we were living on less than two hundred dollars a month, you never complained. That was when I knew that you were a most understanding wife."

Meg's cheeks turned pink as she swallowed hard, and she smiled at Albert. She was thinking how, back then, she had not always considered herself so understanding. But since Albert had just told her how understanding he had always thought she was, she would just keep her own view of herself to herself. Anyway, she knew that since Albert believed it, she was going to go ahead now and really try to become the single most understanding wife in the world!

The use of assets can be just as effective in the business setting as it is in personal life. In many organizations managers have to deal with problems such as high personnel turnover, absenteeism, personality conflicts, reduced productivity and even deliberate subversion of company interests. They often don't realize how they unintentionally have been at least partly responsible for causing the problem by using negative reinforcement.

Negative reinforcement punishes undesirable behavior and leaves the person feeling controlled and coerced. Positive reinforcement rewards desirable behavior and gives the person the feeling that he has some control over what happens to him. It appeals to the better part of his motivations, to his ego.

There's nothing wrong with appealing to someone's ego. Although ego is sometimes viewed with a jaundiced eye, it is still only a three-letter word and a good thing to have around. It is ego, after all, that tells each of us that we can be better than we are and that inspires us to prove that we are really as good as we thought we could be.

It's so easy to find fault; we have all experienced plenty of that. But when someone joins us and sides with our ego, we feel challenged to become as good as we—and they—think we can become. That's why people will try to live up to the assets you see in them.

You have probably had the experience of getting a performance review on which you were told nine wonderful things about yourself, and then one you needed to work on. What did you do with that *but?* You probably spent a lot more time on that one negative than you did on the nine positives. As a matter of fact, if somebody asked you three weeks later what happened at your performance review, you would probably mention that one liability and never mention the nine assets.

And yet aren't companies actually paying people for a job well done? Sure they are, and so you're supposed to know that you are doing a good job because you keep getting a paycheck. Right? We don't think so.

That's not good enough, especially in today's world. We believe that you should know you are doing a good job because somebody is *telling* you that you are. The ramifications of that simple statement are tremendous.

It has been shown that praise is a source of fresh energy. In one demonstration a specially devised mechanism was used to measure the level of energy in children who were performing certain tasks. It was found that when someone gave a tired child an encouraging message, that child's energy level rose dramatically. When something discouraging was said, the child's energy level took a dramatic plunge.

Praise is also an element of creativity. Researchers conducted a study in an average public school in an average American city. They selected a random group of students ranging from the dullest to the brightest but told the teachers that all the children were of the highest intelligence.

When they retested these children a year later, this special group's average IQ had increased from two to twenty-five points—well beyond the gains made by other students. The only difference was that the teachers of the special group expected the children to do well, gave them special attention, encouraged them and treated them with respect.

It isn't really surprising to find someone living up to expectations based upon perceived assets. It seems that when we give someone a higher estimation of himself, he will join us in the work of achieving it.

Sara L. was a successful executive and management consultant, an expert on every phase of behavior modification. But she was having a seemingly intractable problem with her secretary, Amanda P. While Sara was having lunch one day with an associate in the same field, she said, "I have to do something very unpleasant this afternoon."

"What is it?" her friend inquired.

"My secretary is very good, and I hate to lose her," Sara said, "but she is creating too many problems in the office. She arrives late every morning, always with an excellent excuse. She calls in sick so often that by March she had already used up all her sick time for the entire year. She's always needed at home because her children are sick or because there's some problem she has to take care of. Her personal life is totally disorganized. I have talked and talked and talked to her about these things. Last month I finally resorted to documenting her poor performance, showed it to her and gave her a warning that she might be fired. For the next two weeks she improved tremendously. The whole office began to function more efficiently. It was great, for as long as it lasted.''

"What happened?'' Jackie asked.

"It all fell apart again,'' Sara said with a sigh. "She began to slip. Once again she has all these legitimate excuses. But the fact remains that there is a certain amount of time and productivity that the company has a right to expect. I have tried everything, and much as I hate to do it, I'm going to have to fire her today.''

"You're sure that you've tried everything you know?'' Jackie asked. Sara nodded. Then Jackie said, "What did you say to her during the two weeks she was performing so well?''

Sara looked stricken as the light of realization came into her eyes. "Oh, my gosh, I was so busy with the new account!''

"Did anyone reinforce your secretary's improved behavior?''

"I told my assistant, and my assistant told Amanda that she was doing a good job.''

"But *you* didn't.''

Sara laughed and said, "I should know better, right?''

She went back and started all over again with Amanda, this time making sure to reinforce her, and *tell* her, and give her some deserved pats on the back.

While people can be relied upon to react positively to a sincere compliment, they are seldom fooled by flattery. Flattery is based on inflated estimates of character and personality traits. People will usually sense the ulterior motive that lies behind it and be turned off by it. A typical illustration of this is when parents see their children react badly to "praise.''

"It seems that the minute I say, 'You're always such a good boy,' he deliberately sets out to prove that he isn't,'' Michael's mother says. "I'm going to stop telling him he's a good boy if that's all that's going to come of it.''

In a way, Michael's mother is on the right track: if she stops telling Michael he's a good boy and gives him some realistic standards, he'll start living up to them. At least he'll try. But Michael can't handle so broad an evaluation, and he reacts in a way that says, "Oh, no, I'm not always a good boy, and we both know I can't always be because the definition keeps changing." So Michael would rather be praised for specific accomplishments, for what he *does*, rather than for his personality. Adults would rather be praised for their accomplishments, too. They would rather be given an aim, a goal that they can move toward.

Most of us find flattering statements not only embarrassing but also useless. "You're the sweetest, most wonderful little angel to do this for me" is fine between consenting adults in private, but not at the office, please! We have trouble translating that into an asset. How could we honestly say, "Thank you for telling me that I am a sweet, wonderful little angel"? As we try to record something like that on our assets list, modesty would command that part of us would be thinking, I hope nobody checks this too closely.

Praise that relates to accomplishments rather than character or personality is easier to accept, internalize and believe and begin to live up to.

If you can mention assets such as "You turn your assignments in on time," or "You pitch in when there's extra work to be done," then the other person can respond, "Thank you for noticing that," or "Thank you for letting me know that my work is appreciated." When you say to someone, "I appreciate your staying late to get this work done," that person can hear the implied asset: "I am doing a good job." When you say, "Your presentation was very well put together," that person hears the implied asset: "I am capable." When you say, "The ideas that you brought up at the meeting today were very interesting," that person hears the implied asset: "I am original and creative." When the other person can translate what you say into the possession of an asset, then he feels sincerely complimented, recognized for what he has done and patted on the back. That sincere compliment, based on real abilities and accomplishments, is what gives others the motivation, the urge, to do it again and to do it better, in order to receive more praise. Praise is the mightiest of motivators, because we all need it.

Feedback assumes the utmost importance if you are going to motivate people and get good results with them. With all the criticism that's always going around, you won't ever have to worry about somebody being spoiled by too many well-deserved compliments. People can handle that. It's a lack of any feedback that will cause trouble. When people have no clues that specify agreement or disagreement, approval or disapproval, you can be fairly certain that out of all possible choices, they will make negative interpretations. That implied negative input can be just as destructive to enthusiasm as the real thing. So give feedback. Tell them, now.

One way to start doing this is to walk up to somebody and say, "I have never told you this before, but I have always admired you for your ability to . . ." It may be sort of startling at first, and some people may find it very difficult to take because they simply have trouble accepting compliments. But if you're consistent about doing this over a period of time, it will begin to take effect.

Another technique is to say, "I have an ongoing assignment, and I need to find out what two or three of my greatest assets are." Hardly anyone can resist an "I really need your help" kind of appeal. And when you say that to someone you haven't been getting along with, you force the person to look at you in a new light: a positive one. Then, after they have told you what they see as your assets, you could tell them about their assets. As fellow human beings, we all share a need to feel that we have some significance to others, and we all tend to like people who make us feel good about ourselves.

Once in a while in this less-than-ideal world filled with less-than-perfect people, mistakes happen and credit is not given where credit is due. At times like that you have to be satisfied to know for yourself that you are ticking right. In business and in life, sometimes we may have to let someone else take the credit. Sometimes it will involve letting the boss look good when he doesn't even realize that we've done the job he's taking credit for. It's not the kind of thing that should be overdone, but sometimes we're the only ones who knew what we did.

To succeed at any of this, you have to have an unselfish attitude to begin with, which makes you willing to come outside yourself, to turn your focus on other people and to give them honest positive reinforcement by using their assets.

It has to become part of you. You have to realize intellectually that at this particular moment it is your game and your challenge to look at somebody and really see that person's assets, without too much mental twisting and convoluting.

With time and consistent practice it becomes easier and easier, until it becomes almost second nature and you don't have to think about it anymore. You begin to look at people and automatically mention assets, and you begin to become a more positive person yourself. Obviously if you can visualize somebody else's good qualities, you can visualize your own, too.

The more you can enjoy being a giver of assets, the more of a daily habit it will become to use other people's assets to motivate them and to modify their behavior. Practically before you know it, it will have become one of the top items on your own assets list.

Conclusion

There are at least eleven different scientific theories about how human language developed. But there is only one reason: we talk because we have a need to be heard; because we want recognition and understanding from our fellows. And the best route we have is through what we say and how we say it.

This century we live in has been shaken by an almost incredible communications explosion. But while all this change has taken place at the public level, privately we seem less and less able to communicate with each other. On the personal level we *talk* more and more and *communicate* less and less.

We are indeed creatures of habit, as the old saying goes. As we grow from childhood to maturity, we learn certain ways of doing things by repeating them again and again, for months or years or a lifetime, until they become automatic. Unfortunately we also learn some antisuccess habits. Those habits may feel like a natural part of us, but we are not born with them; we acquire them. That means that we can take the initiative to change them, getting rid of the ones that don't serve us well and taking on new ones that will serve us better. Just as skills of all kinds are learned by repetition, in the same way we can unlearn the bad habits and replace them with good ones that can bring us closer to our goals for success.

Change doesn't come easily, but the road to success seldom runs smooth anyway. If you don't underestimate your potential and if you set reasonable goals for yourself, you can move steadily toward those goals, using the techniques in this book as part of your plan.

Planning is important, because if you're not sure where you're going, you won't know how to get there and you may not be able to recognize it when you arrive.

Whether or not you will succeed—and to what degree—we cannot say. It is up to you. But we believe that if someone is determined to succeed, he can. It is within each person's control to do so.

You have covered a great deal of ground with us in this book, raising your awareness of how we listen to each other and of how we talk to each other. Now it is time to take stock and start on the way toward improving your communications. Now it is time to begin to *speak the language of success.*